Nicholas Rescher
Cosmos and Logos
Studies in Greek Philosophy

TOPICS IN ANCIENT PHILOSOPHY
Themen der antiken Philosophie

Herausgegeben von / Edited by

Ludger Jansen • Christoph Jedan • Christof Rapp

Band 1 / Volume 1

Nicholas Rescher

COSMOS AND LOGOS

Studies in Greek Philosophy

ontos

verlag

Frankfurt I Paris I Ebikon I Lancaster I New Brunswick

Bibliographic information published by Die Deutsche Bibliothek
Die Deutsche Bibliothek lists this publication in the Deutsche Nationalbibliographie;
detailed bibliographic data is available in the Internet at http://dnb.ddb.de

North and South America by
Transaction Books
Rutgers University
Piscataway, NJ 08854-8042
trans@transactionpub.com

United Kingdom, Ire, Iceland, Turkey, Malta, Portugal by
Gazelle Books Services Limited
White Cross Mills
Hightown
LANCASTER, LA1 4XS
sales@gazellebooks.co.uk

©2005 ontos verlag
P.O. Box 15 41, D-63133 Heusenstamm nr Frankfurt
www.ontosverlag.com

ISBN 3-937202-65-X

2005

Printed on acid-free paper
ISO-Norm 970-6

Printed in Germany
by dd-ag, Frensdorf-Birkach

PREFACE

Already during my college years in the 1940's, Greek philosophy was one of my early academic loves. Since then, working at the rather sedate pace of a paper or two per decade, I have produced over the past years a handful of studies in the field which, in a small way, reflect my affection for this fascinating field of study. The present book collects these together as a token of historical piety towards the Greek greats in whose footsteps all of us who labor in the vineyard of philosophy continue to tread.

I am grateful to Estelle Burris for her help in preparing this material for print.

Pittsburgh PA
January 2005

Contents

Preface

Chapter 1: Cosmic Evolution in Anaximander

1. Introduction   1
2. The Apeiron   2
3. Process   4
4. Cosmogony   6
5. Cosmology   14
6. Return to and Rebirth from Apeiron   21
7. Conclusion   23

Chapter 2: Contrastive Opposition in Early Greek Philosophy

1. Introduction   33
2. Elements and Opposites   33
3. Proliferating and Arithmetizing Opposites: Pythagoras 34
4. Relativizing Opposites: Xenophanes of Colophon   36
5. Normativizing Opposites: Heraclitus   37
6. Partitioning (and Mixing) Opposites: Anaxagoras   38
7. Empedocles   39
8. Plato   39
10. Aristotle   40
11. Summary   43

Chapter 3: Thought Experimentation in Presocratic Philosophy

1. Introduction: Thought Experiments   47
2. Thales of Miletus   48
3. Anaximander of Miletus   50
4. The Pythagoreans   53
5. Xenophanes of Colophon   53
6. Heraclitus of Ephesus   56
7. Coda   60

Chapter 4: Greek Scepticism's Debt to the Sophist

1. Introduction   63
2. The Phenomena: The Ten Sceptical Tropes of Aenesidemus   63
3. The Main Conclusions Drawn from the Phenomena   67
4. Expansions: The Pervasiveness of the Sophists' Scepticism   71
5. Greek Sophistical Doctrine   74
6. Theory and Practice in Scepticism and Sophistry   76
7. The Promise of Rhetoric: *Nomos* vs. *Phusis*   78
8. Language and its Problems   80
9. Conclusion: How Innovative Were the Greek Sceptics?   83

Chapter 5: Anaximander, Aristotle, and "Buridan's Ass"

1. Introduction   89
2. The Problem   90
3. The History of the Problem of "Buridan's Ass"   92
4. Choice in the Absence of Preference   99
5. A Postscript on Philosophical Issues   104

Chapter 6: Aristotle on Ecthesis and Apodeitic Syllogisms

1. Introduction   115
2. The Technical Situation   116
3. Scientific Demonstration   120
4. Ecthesis   122
5. Conclusion   124

Chapter 1

COSMIC EVOLUTION IN ANAXIMANDER

1. INTRODUCTION

The fragmentary and disjointed nature of the evidence regarding the doctrines of the Milesian philosophers makes it inevitable that any meaningful and cohesive exposition of their thought will be in the nature of an interpretative restoration of the original teaching. By an "interpretative restoration" of a theory, I mean an informative and plausible account of what may reasonably be taken to be its content, and which, while necessarily in some respects conjectural, is at once intrinsically plausible, and adequate to the textual evidence available in the surviving sources. The aim of the present chapter is to provide just this sort of interpretation regarding one aspect of Anaximander's thought: his theory of the nature of the universe and his answer to the abiding questions of how it came in the past to be as it now is, and what is to become of it in the future.

In this attempted restoration of Anaximander's cosmology and cosmogony, primary reliance will be placed on the handful of ancient reports about his teaching that are available to us. No attempt will be made to engage in a systematic critique of various modern interpretations of Anaximander's thought; reference to them will be made only as required to bolster some really critical point of interpretation required for the present account.

In dealing with the teachings of Anaximander, one treads on ground that is at once small and has long been intensively cultivated. It is not easy here to come upon something which is fundamentally new. The major novelty of the ensuing presentation of Anaximander's cosmology is indicated by the expression "cosmic evolution." This chapter traces Anaximander's views on cosmogony in a more detailed way than is usual in presentations of his thought. Insofar as it succeeds in this reconstruction of his teachings, it demonstrates that Anaximander in the sixth century B.C. had an evolutionary concept of the development of the cosmos under the operative agency of familiar natural processes that is more detailed, more "scientific," and vastly more sophisticated than has generally been suspected.

2. THE APEIRON

Simplicius reports that the *apeiron* of Anaximander "is neither water nor any of the things called elements; but the *apeiron*, from which come all the heavens and the worlds in them, is of a different nature. . . . When he (Anaximander) sees the four elements changing into one another, he does not deem it right to make any one of these the *hypokeimenon*, but something else besides them" (A 9.1).[1]   Aristotle correspondingly writes that the reason for taking the *arche* to be "an unlimited something different from the elements" must be that "air is cold, water moist, and fire hot, so that an infinity (*apeiron*) of any one of them would mean that the others would have perished by this time; this, it is said, would not apply to a (neutral) something out of which they all (i.e., the elements) came" (A 16.4).   Again, Aetios reports that Anaximander "fails to say what the *apeiron* is, whether it is air or water or earth, or some other thing" (A 14.1, cf. Diogenes, A 1).   Simplicius quotes Theophrastus as saying that the *apeiron* "is of an indefinite (*aoristos*) nature as regards . . . form" (A 9a). From these reports we may conclude that Anaximander denies specific qualitative definition to the *apeiron*.

This inference is further substantiated by persistent characterizations of the *apeiron* as a *mixture*.   Thus Theophrastus reports that the *apeiron* is conceived by Anaximander as a "mixture of all things (*mixis ton hapaton*)" (Simplicius, A 9a). And this description is also employed by Aristotle and Aetios (A 9.3 and A 17a, respectively).[2]   This "mixture" is not, however, a compound of distinctive elements (such as a mixture of salt and sand), but is a wholly homogeneous and undifferentiated composition (like a mixture of water and wine, or of hot and cold water) in which the "constituent" factors do not exist in any differentiable or discriminable way. Correspondingly Aristotle (A 16.2) and Alexander of Aphrodisias (A 16.1) speak of Anaximander's *apeiron* as something *intermediate* in nature between the elements.

But if the *apeiron* is some sort of mixture, what are its "constituents"? They are the traditional *opposites* (hot/cold, moist/dry).   Thus Simplicius writes that "generation takes place . . . by separation; for the opposites existing in the substance which is infinite matter[3] are separated, according to Anaximander" (A 9.2, or rather, its context in Simplicius' text), and again that "things come into being . . . by the separation of opposites" (A 9.1). Aristotle tells us that Anaximander is among those who "extract out of the one (*arche*) the opposites which inhere in it" (A 16.3, cf. also A 9.3). Correspondingly, Aetios reports, somewhat more definitely, that "Anaximander said that the heavens come to be from a mixture of heat and cold" (A 17a) and Plutarch confirms this, saying that Anaximander taught that "the development of the world began with a separation of heat and cold from the *apeiron*" (A 10). The *apeiron* of Anaximander is thus an undifferentiated—and therefore uncharacterizable—"mixture" in which nothing is in fact discriminable, but in which potentially separable factors, specifically the opposites, are present in a state of mutual neutralization.

Theophrastus wrote that Anaximander viewed the *apeiron* as being "of an indefinite (*aoristos*) nature as regards both form *and magnitude*" (Simplicius, A 9a). And Aristotle's discussion also leaves no doubt that the *apeiron* is boundless with regard to its quantitative, i.e., spatial, extent (A 14.3, A 15). We must conclude that no definite boundaries or limits apply to the *apeiron*, so that it lacks any quantitative as well as any qualitative definition. This aspect of the *apeiron* as a spatial "boundless" leaves open two possibilities: (1) that is is *strictly infinite* in its extension in space, or (2) that it is of finite spatial extent, but without any definite limits, like a fog bank, or the warmth of a fire, or certain clouds. Aristotle (A 15) and writers of his school (e.g., Aetios, A 14.1) interpret Anaximander's *apeiron* in the former sense. However, the evidence available to us—including even that presented in support of this view— does not actually suffice to warrant any decisive choice between these alternatives, so that a decision cannot be made upon textual grounds, but is possible only in the context of a comprehensive concept of Anaximander's world-system. It is my judgment (based upon considerations of this latter kind, as will be seen below) that Anaximander's *apeiron* is limitless or boundless, but not literally infinite.[4]

Besides its role as *arche* or *Urstoff*, the ultimate material source of all existence, the *apeiron* is also an *Urzustand*, a primeval state in the history of the cosmos, from which all subsequent definitions could and did take place. It is that "from which came all the heavens and the world in them" and the "source from which all things arise" (Simplicius, A 9.1). It is the "sole cause of all generations and destruction, and from it all the heavens were separated" (Plutarch, A 10). It precedes all differentiations and in it all things come into being (Hermes, A 12, cf. Hippolytus, A 11).

However, this primeval condition was not wholly abolished with the development of the cosmos, for it is "eternal and imperishable" (Hippolytus, A 11, and see B 1 and B 2). It exists even now, not here *inside* our cosmos, to be sure, but in such a manner as to *surround* the world (Hippolytus, A 11). In due course, the world will cease to exist, and will once again become reabsorbed in the *apeiron* (Simplicius, A 9).[5]

Of the aspects of Anaximander's *apeiron* here considered, two are generally familiar and well understood: (1) its role as the undifferentiated material source of existence (*arche, Urstoff*), and (2) its function as the spatially extended "boundless" within which cosmic development has taken place.[6] However for the purpose of the present investigation, a third aspect of the *apeiron* is of especial importance: its role as the *primeval would-state* from which the process of cosmic development set out. This, in effect, is the *combination* of the two previous features of the *apeiron*. For the first state of the world, according to Anaximander, is one of dominance or pervasion, throughout the spatial "boundless," of a state of "undifferentiated" chaos, making up a condition of primeval *apeiron* (cf. Hesiod, *Theogony*, 116).[7] To see what is involved here, and to understand how Anaximander conceived this primeval world-state of the *apeiron* to give rise to an orderly and differentiated universe, a *cosmos*, we must next consider the place of *process* in Anaximander's cosmogony.

3. PROCESS

Separation. In the physical system of Anaximander, all process is conceived of as *separation* (*ekkrinesis, apokrinesis*). The world thus came into being in consequence of a separation of "the opposites" from the *apeiron*, for as Aristotle tells us in the *Physics*, Anaximander taught that "opposites are separated from the unity" (A 9.3). Simplicius writes that Anaximander "does not think that things come into being by change in the nature of the element, but by the separation of the opposites" (A 9.1). It is this separation from the *apeiron* that inaugurates the development of the cosmos. Plutarch reports that Anaximander "says that the *apeiron* is the sole cause of all generation and destruction, and from it the heavens were separated" (A 10), and again that "at the beginning of the world something productive of heat and cold from the eternal being [i.e., the *apeiron*] was separated therefrom" (A 10).

Our most suggestive information as to what is involved in Anaximander's concept of separation comes from the doxographic discussions of his ideas on meteorology. Here the fundamental concept is through-out that of modifications of vapor (*atmos*). Thus wind "is due to a *separation (apokrinesis)* of the lightest vapors and the motion of the masses of these vapors" (Hippolytus, A 11). Again, "moisture comes from the vapor raised by the sun" (Hippolytus, A 11), as with rain, or dew, or perspiration.[8] Lightning occurs "when a wind falls upon clouds and *separates* them" (Hippolytus, A 11), and thunder is the noise caused by their being broken apart (Aetios, A 23.1).

This process of separation of vapors, or some very close analogue to it, is operative throughout Anaximander's physics. Thus the sun and moon "revolve by reason of vapors and exhalations, and revolve in those regions where they found an abundance of them" (Alexander, A 27.2), "The sea is what is left of the first moisture" and "it diminishes in quantity, being evaporated gradually by the sun, and finally it will be completely dried up" (Alexander, A 27.2). All of our information on Anaximander indicates that the basic modification of vapor—rarefaction, compression (as with bellows), exhalations, winds, etc.—as well as changes to and from a vaporous state through evaporation and condensation, are the basic principles of explanation throughout the natural philosophy of Anaximander.[9] Aristotle ranks Anaximander among the physicists "who hold that the *hypokeimenon* is *one* kind of substance . . . and arrive at plurality by conceiving all else to be generated from it by condensation and rarefaction" (A 16.2). Even man's soul "is like air in its nature" (Aetios, A 19). All of these modifications of vapor can be taken as species of Anaximander's genus *separation*. Here lies the truth of Seneca's report: *Anaximandrus omnia ad spiritum retulit* (A 23.2). (Just this makes the step from the system of Anaximander to that of Anaximentes at once short and natural.)

The Eternal Motion. What is the root cause of the various types of separation; what starts off the series of separations that get the cosmogonic process under way? This causal agency of creation in the system of Anaximander is *motion*—or rather, one particular mode of motion, coeternal with the *apeiron*, the "eternal motion." This is an entirely natural agency, wholly random, unplanned and undirected, so that Augustine's remark that Anaximander did not "attribute any place to divine mind in the scheme of things" (A 17.1) is quite in order.

Simplicius writes, that Anaximander "does not think that things come into being by change in the nature of the element, but by separation of the opposites, which the eternal motion causes" (A 9.1). Again, we are told that, according to Anaximander, "motion is eternal, and as a result of it the heavens arise" (Hippolytus, A 11), and that "motion is eternal, for without motion there would be no coming to be or passing away" (Simplicius, A 17.6). This background renders intelligible the somewhat garbled report of Hermes: "Anaximander says that the first principle is older than water, and is eternal motion—in this all things come to be and all things perish" (A 12).

No information has come down to us as to how Anaximander conceived of this "eternal motion." Its description becomes a matter of conjecture and interpretation. We have seen above that the *apeiron* is to be considered as an undifferentiated, chaotic (vaporous)[10] stuff filling the universe in its primitive state. Presumably, however, the primordial "eternal motion" is to be viewed as a wholly chaotic and haphazard multitude of winds and currents stirring at random in the (vaporous) *apeiron*. In the course of these haphazard movements, it eventually chances that an eddy happens to form. And with this primeval whirlwind or cosmic *dinê*, the processes of separation leading to the development of an orderly universe, or cosmos, begin to get under way.[11]

4. COSMOGONY

It is clear from our evidence that, according to the conception of Anaximander, the world has reached its present state of definition as the result of a process of development, passing through a series of distinct stages. We have, unfortunately, not one comprehensive and explicit report on the details of the Anaximandrean cosmogony. However, the doxographic reports that have come down suffice to make an interpretation possible which reconstructs Anaximander's theory of cosmic evolution, and which permits a detailed characterization of his teachings regarding the present constitution of the resultant cosmos. Such a reconstruction is presented in this section and the following one.

Stage I. As already indicated, Anaximander holds that the primordial state or condition that exists prior to the outset of cosmic development is that of the *apeiron*. In it obtains a state of "mixture" prior to all *separation*, a universal chaos in which nothing has acquired definite qualitative definition, nor is any definite boundary to be assumed to give a quantitative limitation to its extent. In this primordial *apeiron* only the agency of the *eternal motion* is already at work; random gusts of wind stirring, as it were, in the undifferentiated bleakness. This first stage is

Figure 1

Stage I. *The Apeiron*

depicted diagrammatically in the representation of Figure 1. Here the enclosure has been drawn as a zigzag in order to avoid conveying the idea of a definite quantitative limit, while at the same time not insisting on a strictly infinite extent. With this state of complete rule of the *apeiron* we have set the stage upon which the cosmogonic drama is to be played.

The causal agency in this drama of world development is the *eternal motion*, that chaotic stirring indicated in the diagram by means of wavy lines. Due to its operation it chances that an eddy (*dinê*) is formed, quite fortuitously, in the *apeiron*. With this, a process of *separation* is inaugurated, as we shall shortly see; a process that effects a transition to another world-state, the first way-station on the road of cosmic development.

Stage II. According to a report of Alexander of Aphrodisias, Theophrastos said that Anaximander taught that "the sea is what is left of the first moisture; for when the region about the earth[12] was moist, the upper part of the moisture was evaporated by the sun" (A 27.2). Again, Aetios reports that "Anaximander held that the sea is the remainder of the original flooding, the fire has for the most part dried this up . . ." (A 27.3; cf. Aristotle, A 27.1). These statements suggest that Anaximander believed that at a primitive stage of cosmic evolution there was a separation of opposites: a cold and wet core of *moisture* (the "original flooding") being formed at the center of the world, and this surrounded by a hot and dry envelopment of *fire*. Just this description is the scope of Plutarch's report that, according to Anaximander, "at the beginning of the world, something productive of heat and cold from the eternal being [the *apeiron*] was separated therefrom, and a sort of sphere of this flame surrounded . . . [the center of the world] as bark surrounds a tree" (A 10). This separation of moisture and fire is the first stage of *definition* in the development of the cosmos, after the primordial monotony of the *apeiron*. Aetios thus tells us that "Anaximander said that the heavens come to be from a mixture of heat and cold" (A 17a).

But how does this separation of fire and moisture come about? Here—in the absence of any explicit reports—we must rely upon indirect evidence and interpretation. The key to this is the recognition that Anaximander regards fire as a form of (light) vapor. Thus Anaximander is said to have held that the sun "sends out fire through a narrow opening, like the air from a flute" (Aetios, A 21.2), that "as from a trumpet it [the sun] sends forth its light . . . like a bellows" (Achilles, A 12.1), and that the sun "sends forth exhalations" and an eclipse takes place "when the outlet for the fiery exhalations is closed" (Aetios, A 21.4). The sun and the moon "make their revolutions by reason of vapors and exhalations, and revolve in those regions where they find an abundance of them" (Alexander, A 27.2). The stars are "wheel-shaped masses of air, full of fire, breathing out flames from pores" (Aetios, A 18.1). In short, Anaximander conceived of fire on so close an analogy with air that we are justified in inferring that for him fire was a light form of vapor.

This is the key to understanding the *separation* of moisture and fire caused by the *eternal motion*, once it brings about a whirlwind or eddy (*dinê*). The light vapors of fire naturally tend toward the periphery of the eddy, leaving behind concentrated at the center heavier vapors that make up the *moisture*. This process can be illustrated from Plato's subsequent discussion of cosmic development from chaos in the *Timaeus*:[13]

> [The primordial chaos] had every sort of diverse appearance to the sight; but because it was filled with powers that were neither alike nor evenly balanced, there was no equipoise in any region of it; but it was everywhere swayed unevenly and shaken by these things, and by its motion shook them in turn. And they, being thus moved, were perpetually being separated and carried in different directions; just as when things are shaken and winnowed by means of winnowing-baskets and other instruments for cleaning corn, the dense and heavy things go one way, while the rare and light are carried to another place and settle there. In the same way the four kinds [elements] were shaken by the Recipient [the containing matrix], which itself was in motion like an instrument for shaking, and it separated the most unlike kinds farthest

Figure 2

Stage II: *Separation of Moisture and Fire*

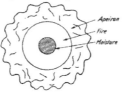

apart from one another, and thrust the most alike together; whereby the different kinds came to have different regions, even before the ordered whole consisting of them came to be. Before that, all these kinds were without proportion or measure. (*Timaeus*, 52 D.)

The second step in the development of the cosmos, accordingly, is one of separation of moisture (wet and cold) from fire (dry and hot), with a "sort of sphere" of flame surrounding the moist center or core. This second stage may be depicted diagrammatically as per Figure 2. Here fire and moisture have become separated, inaugurating a process of evaporation or drying-up (again *separation*) which continues to make for the further differentiations of cosmic developments.[14]

It is to be noted that this initiation of the cosmogonic process does *not* abolish the *apeiron*, but merely *relegates* it into the background by exiting it into the outer regions, as it were. It continues in unmodified existence, as is shown in the diagram, in such a manner as to *surround* or *envelop* the central sphere that is the realm in which the drama of cosmic evolution unfolds. This accords with the relevant testimony of our sources. Thus Hippolytus writes that the *apeiron* "is eternal and does not grow old, and it surrounds all the worlds" (A 11). And Aristotle records that Anaximander wrote that the *apeiron* is "immortal and indestructable" and that it "embraces and governs" the world (A 15).[15]

Figure 3

Stage III, Phase I: *The Origin of Air*

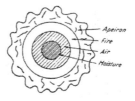

It is therefore incorrect to view the *apeiron* solely as an *Urstoff* which is used up or transformed in the process of cosmic creation. It continues to exist, in the background, as it were, in an unchanged way, enveloping the cosmos.[16]   Indeed, the *apeiron*, as we shall see, bides its time, tolerating the intrusion of a differentiated cosmos for only some finite span of time, and then closing in once again and reabsorbing it, once the processes of separation have played themselves out, as they inevitably must.

Stage III. According to a report of Theophrastus, Anaximander held that "the upper part of the moisture was evaporated by the sun, and from it came the winds . . ." (Alexander, A 27.2). Aetios says that Anaximander held that "wind is a current in the air, in which the finest and moistest parts are set in motion by the sun or are melted down" (A 24). Similarly, Anaximander is said to have taught that "winds are due to a separation of the lightest vapors and the motion of the masses of these vapors; and moisture comes from the vapors raised by the sun from them" (Hippolytus, A 11). Again, Alexander of Aphrodisias tells us that the three primary items to have emerged from the *apeiron* are fire, water, and air (A 16.1).

It appears therefore that the next step in the process of cosmic development, according to the conception of Anaximander, is one in which fire, by "separating the lightest vapors" from the primordial moisture, bring *air* (and with it wind) into existence, leaving the moisture in a state of increased concentration, the "lightest vapors" having been drawn off from it.   This suggests a resultant state as represented in Figure 3.   This representation is, however, in need of amendment. With the generation of air, a *separation* takes place in the circle of fire—apparently it finds a

Figure 4

Stage III, Phase 2: *Circles of Fire*

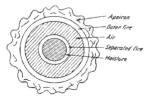

Figure 5

Stage IV, Phase 1: *A Dualization of Air*

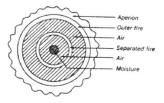

weakness in the air barrier and rushes inwards (a tendency of which more later.) In such a manner the region of fire is split into *two* circles, one of which continues to surround the inner core of moisture, and is separated from the outer circle of fire by the newly created circle of air. We learn of this development from a report of Hippolytus, who speaks of "a circle of fire, separated from the fire about the world . . ." (A 11). And again, Plutarch reports that the "sphere of flame" was "broken into parts and defined into distinct circles" (A 10). This brings us to Figure 4.

And so, as the fire continues to work upon the interior moisture, drying it up, and creating a second layer of air around the inner core of moisture. This produces exactly the situation described by Hippolytus as "a circle of fire, separated from the fire about the world, and surrounded by air" (A

Figure 6

Stage IV, Phase 2: *The Origin of the Earth*

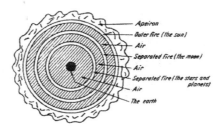

11). This stage of cosmic evolution, may be represented diagrammatically in Figure 5.

Stage IV. The fourth and final act of the drama of creation in the cosmogony of Anaximander involves two steps: (1) a drying-up—due to the intense heat of the outer fire—of the central core of moisture, separating it into an almost solid inner core (the earth) associated with residual moisture, its seas, surrounded by air (a semi-moist medium), and (2) a repetition of the Stage III process, producing a second splitting in the outer ring of fire, again dividing it into two rings separated from one another by air. The diagrammatic representation of the structure of resultant cosmos is as pictured in Figure 6. As indicated in the diagram, the three fiery rings are associated with the stars and planets, the moon, and the sun, in order of increasing distance from the earth. Further discussion of this astronomical aspect of Anaximander's cosmology must be deferred; we have first to examine the textual evidence for the two processes that have supposedly brought us to this fourth and, to date, final stage of Anaximander's cosmogony, viz., the development of the earth through drying-up, and the second separation within the ring of fire.

There is a great deal of evidence that Anaximander held that a continued drying-up and evaporation of the primordial moisture brought the earth into existence. Thus Theophrastos reports that, according to Anaximander, "the sea is what is left of the first moisture; for when the region about the earth was moist, the upper part was evaporated by the sun

. . .; what is left of this moisture in the hollow places [of the earth] is the sea; so it diminishes in quantity, being dried up gradually by the sun, and finally it will be completely dried up" (Alexander, A 27.1). Again, Aetios tells us that "Anaximander held that the sea is the remainder of the original flooding, the fire has for the most part dried this up, and has changed the rest through the drying-up" (27.3), and Aristotle writes that Anaximander taught that "originally the earth was enveloped by moisture; then the sun began to dry it up . . . and the remainder forms the sea . . . [which] is being dried up and is growing less, and will end by being some day entirely dried up" (27.1). It is doubtless for this reason" that Anaximander held that "the first animals were generated in the moisture, and were covered with a prickly skin; and as they grew older they became drier and drier and after a while the skin broke off from them . . ." (Aetios, A 30.1). Censorinus says that Anaximander held that, when land and sea separated, "there emerged fish and fish-like animals, and men came to take form in these, and the foetus retained them until puberty, but then the enclosure broke, and men and women capable of nourishing themselves emerged" (A 30.2), and Plutarch correspondingly reports that Anaximander held that "at first men were generated in the form of fishes" (A 30.3). It is thus clear that Anaximander taught that the earth was formed out of the "first moisture" through separation due to evaporation and drying-up.

Anaximander's thesis of the separation of the outer ring of fire into two distinct circles must next be considered. The best report that has come down to us on this aspect of Anaximander's teaching is Plutarch's statement that Anaximander holds that "at the beginning of this world something productive of heat and cold from the eternal being [the *apeiron*] was separated therefrom, and a sort of sphere of flame surrounded the air about the earth . . . and this sphere was broken into parts and defined into distinct circles, and thus arose the sun and the moon and the stars" (A 10). This background clarifies Aetios' report that Anaximander said that the stars are wheel-shaped masses of air, full of fire" (A 18.1), and again that "the circle of the sun . . . is like a chariot wheel, having a hollow center, and this full of fire" (Aetios, A 22.1). We shall return below to a fuller consideration of the meaning of these reports. Here they are adduced solely as furnishing support to the thesis that the original "fire around the world" (Hippolytus, A 11) was split into three distinct and separated circles, giving form to the sun, the moon, and the stars and planets.[17] That it is *air* that separates these rings of fire from each other is further suggested in the statement that "the stars are wheel-shaped masses of air, full of fire" (Aetios, A 21), and this suggestion is fully substantiated in Hippolytus' report that "the stars are a circle of fire separated from the fire about the world [the sun] and surrounded by air" (A 11).

With this fourth stage of development, the cosmogonic process of Anaximander has attained to the universe which we inhabit, as he sees it, a vast complex of cosmic wheels, turning by the residual *dinê*, and thus producing the principal observed astronomical phenomena. Let us now take up a detailed, and indeed quantitive examination of the structure of the universe, according to the theory of Anaximander.

5. COSMOLOGY

In describing the universe of Anaximander, I propose first to consider the earth and its place, then to examine the descriptive aspects of Anaximander's cosmology, and finally to take up the quantitative relationships which he conceives to obtain among the major elements of the cosmos.

The Earth. Anaximander taught that the earth is located in the center of the cosmos (Diogenes, A 1; Suidas, A 2; Theon of Smyrna, A 26.2) A curious line of supporting reasoning as to how the earth is able to maintain itself unsupported in space has attached itself to this belief so early and so consistently as to leave no reasonable doubt that it derives from Anaximander himself. This is given in Hippolytus' report that Anaximander held that "the earth is a heavenly body, controlled by no other power, and keeping its position because it is the same distance from all things" (A 11).[18] The earth is thus able to keep its place solely by virtue of considerations of cosmic symmetry.

The *shape* of the earth is that of a drum, i.e., with cylindrical sides and a flat top and base. In our accounts it is described sometimes as a cylinder (Plutarch, A 10; Hippolytus, A 11), sometimes as a section of a pillar (B 5; Hippolytus, A 11; Aetios, A 25); the latter description having been used by Anaximander himself (B 5). It is probable that Anaximander used the description "like bark surrounds a tree" (Plutarch, A 10) to illustrate how air envelops the earth (as well as to describe the manner in which fire surrounds the air about the earth, as in Plutarch's text). The height of the earth-cylinder was said by Anaximander to be one-third of its breadth (Plutarch, A 10).[19] Thus the structure of the earth, in Anaximander's view, is depicted in Figure 7. Nothing is reported as to Anaximander's beliefs regarding either the sides of the earth or its nether face. However,

Figure 7

Anaximander's Earth

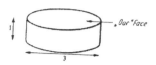

he did describe "our" face, to the extent of making a model or map of it. For this he was celebrated in antiquity as the first map-maker. Agathemeros writes that Anaximander "was the first to draw the inhabited world on a board" and that, after some subsequent modifications, it became "a much-admired thing" (A 6.1; and cf. Strabo, A 6.2).

The Stars and Planets, the Moon, and the Sun. In a passage already quoted, Plutarch reports that Anaximander taught that in the beginning "a sort of sphere of . . . flame surrounded the air around the earth . . . and this sphere was broken into distinct circles, and thus arose the sun and the moon and the stars" (A 10). We have already considered this splitting of the outer fire into three distinct rings. But we must now consider more closely their *function* in the cosmology of Anaximander.

The outermost circle of fire is the sun, the next is that of the moon, and the innermost is that of the stars and planets. Thus Aetios writes that Anaximander taught "that the sun has the highest position of all, the moon is next in order, and beneath it are the fixed stars and the planets" (A 18.2). Now the sun, according to Anaximander, has "the shape of a wheel" (Achilles, A 21.1), it is "like a chariot wheel, having a hollow center, and this is full of fire" (Aetios, A 21.2; cf. *idem*, A 22.1). Thus sun therefore is like a broad wheel without spokes, the rim of the wheel being composed of fire, that is, it is a hollow cylinder, the cylindrical container itself being composed of fire. This wheel of fire is blocked off from the earth by the ring of air which contains and limits it on its inner side, except in one weak spot, through which the fire can escape by breaking through and rushing in earthwards. This is our visible sun. Thus Achilles reports that Anaximander held "that the sun, the source of light, has the shape of a wheel; and just as the center of a wheel is hollow,and from it the spokes go out to the outer rim, so the sun, which sends forth its light from outer space, makes a spoke with its rays, which shine forth from the ring in a circle: as from a trumpet it sends forth its light from a hollow and narrow place, like a bellows" (A 21.1). The revolution of the sun is therefore not due to any motion of its fire-ring, but to the turning of the air-mass within, which revolves and so carries around with it the weak spot through which the fire of the sun-circle can escape.[20]   This is the sense of Alexander of Aphrodisias' statement: "[air came to be] when the upper part of the [primordial] moisture was evaporated by the sun [i.e., the outer fire], and from it came the winds and the revolutions of the sun and moon, since these make their revolutions by reason of the vapors and exhalations" (A 27.2; cf. Aristotle, A 27.1).

Exactly the same description applies to the constitution and to the functioning of the moon circle and the star circle. Thus Hippolytus reports Anaximander to have maintained that: "The stars are a circle of fire . . . surrounded by air. There are certain breathing-holes like the holes of a flute through which we see the stars; so that when the holes are stopped up, there are eclipses. The moon is sometimes full and sometimes in other phases as these holes are stopped up or open" (A 11). Aetios writes; "Anaximander said that the stars are wheel-shaped masses of air, full of fire, breathing out flames from pores in different parts" (A 18.1), and again: "The circle of the moon . . . like the circle of the sun is full of fire, but there is only one exit for the fire. . . . The moon is eclipsed when the hole in the wheel is stopped" (A 22.1 and A 22.2).

On the basis of this information we can amend the description of our diagrammatic representation of Anaximander's cosmology in Figure 6 in the manner indicated in Figure 8. The fire-circles, it should be noted, are removed from the earth in order of increasing brightness. If the brighter rings were closer, the dimmer would be invisible behind them. As to the *apeiron* we are wholly blocked off from it, either by air so thick that we cannot see *through* it, or by fire so intense that we cannot see *past* it. This removes Aristotle's criticism (*Physics*, 204b31) that there cannot be an eternal *apeiron* other than the elements, for if there were, it would have to exist in our world *now*, but no such thing is apparent to observation.

Quantitative Relationships. In antiquity Anaximander was regarded as among the first to essay a mathematical description of the universe. Thus Simplicius says that "Anaximander first expatiated on the arrangement of the planets and on their size and their distance [from the earth]" (A 19), and Suidas says that he "showed that geometry is a pattern of the whole"

Figure 8

Anaximander's Universe

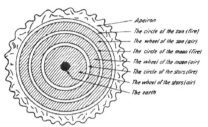

Apeiron
The circle of the sun (fire)
The wheel of the sun (air)
The circle of the moon (fire)
The wheel of the moon (air)
The circle of the stars (fire)
The wheel of the stars (air)
The earth

NOTE: This representation accords with the strict accuracy of Hippolytus' statement that according to Anaximander: "The stars are a circle of fire separated from the fire about the world [i.e., the sun] and surrounded by air [i.e., on both sides]" (A 11).

(A 2). Only a few scraps of information regarding Anaximander's quantitative description of the cosmos have come down to us, and even these contain some conflicts, so that their interpretation has occasioned some difficulty. Here, in a few lines, is the entire body of our evidence on Anaximander's numerical characterizations of astronomical relationships:

The sun is equal in size to the earth, but the circle from which it sends forth its exhalations, and by which it is borne through the heavens, is 27 times as large as the earth. (Aetios, A 213).

The circle of the sun is 28 times as large as that of the earth . . . (Aetios, A 21.2).

The circle of the sun is 27 times as large as that of the moon, but the circles of the fixed stars are lower. (Hippolytus, A 11.)

The circle of the moon is 19 times as large as the earth . . . (Aetios, A 22.1.)

Table 1

Object	Radius	Circumference	Ratio of Circum-ference to Earth's
Earth	1	$2\pi(1)$	1
Moon Circle (Inner Perimeter)	18	$2\pi(18)$	18
Moon Circle (Outer Perimeter)	19	$2\pi(19)$	19
Sun Circle (Inner Perimeter)	27	$2\pi(27)$	27
Sun Circle (Outer Perimeter)	28	$2\pi(28)$	28

The following conclusions are suggested: (1) The (circumference of the) sun-circle is 27 or 28 times as great as the earth's circumference, (2) the circumference of the moon circle is 19 times that of the earth, (3) the circumference of the star-circle(s) is smaller than that of the moon-circle, and (4) the report of Hippolytus is garbled in that it ought to read that the sun-circle is 27 times that of the *earth* (which otherwise serves as basis of reference throughout), and *not* that of the *moon*.

This information strongly suggests the analysis of Table 1.

The fact that Anaximander conceives of the sun as a *ring* whose limiting band is defined by two perimeters, explains how *both* 27 and 28 can be used correctly to characterize its dimensions, as occurs in our reports.[21]

These quantitative relationships indicate that the dimensions of Anaximander's universe are as represented in the Figure 9. The radii, and therefore the circumference of these circles increase in the progression 9 x 1, 9 x 2, 9 x 3, a relationship which is found in various primitive cosmologies.[22]   Here the number 3 is often of special prominence as regards its symbolical significance, and it is thus that is enters into Anaximander's cosmology: here in yielding the factor 9 = 3 x 3, and also above in constituting the ratio of the diameter of the earth-cylinder to its height. It is apparently to such a mystico-numerological origin, rather than to any empirical basis, that the numerical factors in Anaximander's

Figure 9.

The Dimensions of Anaximander's Cosmos

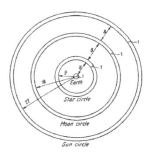

quantitative description of the cosmos must be traced.

The foregoing discussion has considered the structure of the universe on the theory of Anaximander solely with respect to its appearance from *above*, as it were; nothing has so far been said about its appearance viewed *from the side*. This has been so because our reports are virtually silent, yielding no direct information whatever on this head, and little that is indirect. What can be said is therefore almost wholly conjectural. We do, however, have two firm items of information: (1) that our earth is a cylinder whose height is one-third of its breadth (Plutarch, A 10), and (2) that the stars, moon, and sun which surround it are wheel-shaped masses of fire, separated from one another by wheel-shaped masses of air having certain lateral dimensions (see the foregoing discussion). I think that it is a defensible conjecture that Anaximander believed that the wheels of the celestial bodies also had a height that is one-third their breadth, just like the earth, which could put their breadth of their respective wheels into the proportion 1:2:3, or rather more descriptively 3:6:9, measured by a scale with the diameter of the earth-cylinder as a unit. On the basis of this conjecture, we would obtain the view of Anaximander's cosmos, as seen in cross-section from the side, that is given in Figure 10. The manner in which the sun (for example) illuminates the earth is illustrated in the Figure 11. This figure makes clear why the sun-fire must be the most intense, more powerful than that of the moon or star rings, since it must be able to

Figure 10

A Side View of Anaximander's Universe (Conjecture)

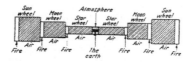

Figure 11

The Transmission of Sunlight

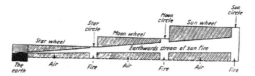

NOTE1: On this conception, there is a real problem as to how the sun, moon, etc., can ever appear directly overhead. Could Anaximander have conceived of a *bending* of the fire streams in their earthwards course, that is, have entertained some idea of *refraction*? More likely, he took the wheels to have varying inclinations to one another, rather than being co-planar.

NOTE2: This diagram of course fails to indicate the periodic "wobble" of this cosmic wheel in its rotation about the earth.

penetrate through them on its route to the earth. As regards the manner of the transmission of their light, the moon and the stars operate in a fashion that is wholly analogous to that of the sun. We thus see why it is important for Anaximander to place the celestial fires at distances from the earth *inverse* to their brightness—because in this way the stronger light can shine through the weaker. (Moreover in a *dinê* the center rotates faster than the periphery, and so this arrangement also accords with the relative

Figure 12

The Movement of Sunlight over the Face of Anaximander's Earth

NOTE: Major seasonal and climatic phenomena would be explainable in terms of a periodic shift of the center of the disk of sunlight, taking it at times nearer to the earth's periphery, and at times further away.

observed transit of the stars, moon, and sun through their daily, monthly, and annual cycles.)

The way in which the rotation of the air-mass causes the light of the sun to move over the flat surface of Anaximander's earth-disk (and analogously for lunar and stellar illumination) is shown in Figure 12.[23] This completes the present discussion of the structure of the universe as it appears to emerge from the reports of the cosmology of Anaximander. We now conclude the examination of Anaximander's views regarding the *present* constitution of the cosmos, and will turn to a look at his views regarding its *future*. (The past has, of course, already been dealt with in the preceding section on cosmogony.)

6. RETURN TO AND REBIRTH FROM THE APEIRON

Return. Our universe, having come into being by a process of development out of the all-embracing prehistoric state of *apeiron*, does not continue in unceasing existence according to the views of Anaximander. For as Aetios reports, "Anaximander . . . taught that the world is perishable" (A 27.5). How does the world perish? the answer is: through a return to the *apeiron*. In the *apeiron* "all things come into being and all things perish" (Hermes, A 12). The *apeiron* is that "from which come all the heavens and the worlds in them; and from what such things arise, to that they return of necessity when they are destroyed, for he

[Anaximander] says that they 'suffer punishment and give satisfaction to one another for injustice according to the order of time,' putting it in rather poetical language" (Simplicius, A 9.1; B 1). "From this [the *apeiron*] all things come and all things perish and return to this" (Aetios, A 14). It is clear, then, that Anaximander taught that the cosmos is destined for destruction and re-absorption to the *apeiron*.

The end of the world and its return to the *apeiron* is inherent in the very nature of Anaximander's fundamental concept of cosmic process. For, ever since our world began to come into being with a primordial *separation* of two opposing factors (the hot-dry and the cold-moist), its entire history has been one of homogenization,[24] through continued separations affecting these opposites, and doing this in such a way as to make for re-uniting of the initially separated factors. For example, the earth's sea "diminishes in quantity, being evaporated gradually by the sun, and finally it will be completely dried up" (Alexander, A 27.2). And the heat of the sun is constantly diminishing, because the sun "as from a trumpet . . . sends forth its light from a hollow and narrow place, like a bellows" (Achilles, A 21). Such processes as evaporation or drying-up, exhalation, condensation, and all the other types of Anaximandrean "separation" are inherently terminating processes. Like the flame that consumes the burning wood, their very operation exhausts the materials requisite to their continuation.

Thus on Anaximander's conception, the whole history of the universe since the initial separation of the hot and the cold that has led to the existence of a cosmos, is one of gradual mutual neutralization of these opposites through continuing separations. To these processes of separation the world owes its existence. But once they have wholly done their work, and have run themselves down, homogeneity will once again dominate over separateness and qualitative distinction. Then the *apeiron* that hovers ever about the boundaries of the cosmos, like a vulture awaiting the death of its prey, will close in once again to claim to itself the once differentiated cosmos to which, in time immemorial, it chanced to give birth.

Rebirth.   The life-span of our orderly universe is finite, and its destruction and return to the all embracing *apeiron* is inevitable. But the *apeiron* itself is "immortal and indestructible" (B 3). Why, therefore, should not another cosmos come to be created? If the "eternal motion" once chanced to inaugurate a process of cosmogony, could this not happen again? These questions reproduce Anaximander's own line of thought and led him to maintain that world creation (emergence from the *apeiron*) and destruction (return to the *apeiron*) are *alternating* phases of cosmic history. "[Anaximander] declared that destruction and, far earlier, generation have taken place since an infinite time, since all things are involved in a cycle" (Plutarch, A 10). Anaximander taught that "there are innumerable worlds in which all things come to pass—these worlds he thought to be now destroyed, now to come again into being, each lasting for whatever time it could" (Augustine, A 17.1). Again, Aetios reports that Anaximander maintained that "from this [the *apeiron*] all things come and all things perish and return to this; accordingly an infinite number of worlds have been generated and have perished again and returned to their source" (A 14.1).[25]

Thus while the destruction of our universe is inevitable, this will not make an end of cosmic history. Precisely because our universe came to be due to the agency of a chance or random process (the eternal motion) it is a certainty that—over the trackless infinitude of time—the drama of cosmic creation will be played again and again.

7. CONCLUSION

The main novelty in the foregoing description of Anaximander's cosmology, and the primary respect in which it is an advance upon the currently accepted accounts, is with regard to its detailed picture of his theory of the genetic constitution of the cosmos, i.e., of Anaximander's cosmogony. I would like in concluding to dwell on one implication of this interpretation: that for Anaximander's standing in the history of science. There is no question that, insofar as the foregoing account is correct, it shows that Anaximander in the sixth century B.C. possessed a conception of the development of the universe in the consequence of natural occurrences and the workings-out of natural processes that is more detailed, more *scientific*, and greatly more sophisticated than has usually been credited.

Even George Sarton has markedly underrated Anaximander's contribution to the development of that endeavor we today call *science*:

Thales' idea that water is the primary substance had much to commend itself, yet it had obvious shortcomings. How could we understand the transformation of water into earth, or wood, or iron? What other principle could one suggest? It is clear that if one had to choose among the kinds of matter familiar to one's senses, ubiquitous and protean water was incomparably the best. Water was the best, yet it would not do. Anaximander saved himself from that corner by taking refuge in an abstraction, in a word. Philosophers, and even a few scientists, have repeated that performance over and over again, to their satisfaction and apparently to the satisfaction of their readers. Anaximander did not abandon the Thalesian idea of the substantial unity of nature, but since no tangible substance could serve us as prime substance (*archê*), he imagined one that was intangible and called it *apeiron*. . . . The primary substance *apeiron* is undetermined because it is potentially everything.[26] . . . [In discussing his cosmology] we need not be very precise in our terminology; so little of his book is available and that little is so unclear and ambiguous that to explain his views with exact terms would be like weighing dirt with a balance of precision. . . . [Anaximander] was neither a scientist nor a metaphysician in the modern sense of those terms. . . . He was the first to state some of the fundamental problems of science; his answers were too bald and premature, but not in their own background irrational.[27]

It appears, quite to the contrary, that Anaximander had devised a theory of the constitution of the universe (elaborated down to quantitative detail in some of its respects) that was capable of providing (1) an explanation of at least the most obvious astronomical and meteorological phenomena of the world as presently constituted, and (2) a strictly *naturalistic* account—in terms of familiar processes—of how the universe came to develop into its present state.

With the cosmology of Anaximander an important formative step in the development of the concept of *scientific explanation* is taken. The entire system of Anaximander is articulated in terms of analogies with familiar natural processes: winds, evaporation, condensation, dew, the compression of air, in bellows or wind instruments, the formation of an eddy (*dinê*) of water, the turning of wheels, etc. Here then we see the inauguration of one of the most fundamental schemata of scientific explanation: the assimilation through analogy of the phenomenon to be explained to one that is already relatively well understood. There are many instances in Anaximander's theory of just this procedure; to cite just one example, consider his conception of the cosmic formation of air from the primordial moisture as thought of an analogy with the boiling off of water over a fire and the evaporation of a pool of water by the heat of the sun.

Anaximander stands prominent among the inaugurators of cosmic uniformitarianism: his is perhaps the first systematic attempt to depict the workings of our universe in terms of ongoing processes thoroughly familiar from the ordinary experience of man's immediate environment.

A second major contribution made by Anaximander's theories to the development of scientific thought is closely related to the foregoing concept of explanation. This is the idea of a "model" for scientific explanation, that is, a complex mechanical analogue whose functioning mirrors the workings of a natural process. This contribution is cogently formulated in S. Sambursky's discussion of Anaximander in his book on *The Physical World of the Greeks*:

> . . . use was made for the first time of the scientific model . . . [for] explaining phenomena . . . . It was also Anaximander who used the mechanical model as a means of demonstrating a physical phenomenon. Even to-day, when absolute precision of terminology and mathematical abstraction rule the natural sciences, it would still seem impossible for science to dispense with the model as a means of giving concrete form to its ideas and methods. From time to time, when we want a concrete illustration of "how things work," we have to put aside mathematical abstractions and the absolute precision of the language of symbols and have recourse to a mechanical model. We form a conception of the action of elastic forces with the aid of springs, or we picture the structure of the molecule in the shape of balls joined together in a certain pattern in space. We explain propagation of sound or electromagnetic radiation by employing the model of water waves in a pool, and at present we are striving to find a suitable model for what happens in the nucleus of an atom. According to the circumstances of the case, we consider the model either as an approximation to reality, or as an exact replica of it, or simply as a makeshift which gives us only an elementary conception of the mechanism of the phenomenon. . . .

Anaximander's use of a mechanical model to illustrate the dimensions and movements of the heavenly bodies was an enormous advance on the allegories and mythological fancies current before his time. "Anaximander said that the sun is a circle twenty-eight times the size of the earth. It is like the wheel of a chariot with a hollow rim full of fire. At a certain point the fire shines out, through an opening like a nozzle of a pair of bellows. . . . An eclipse of the sun results from the closing of the opening through which the fire appears" (Aetios, A 21). . . . The wheel is made of compressed air. Now since water vapour was included in the concept of air, the air wheels are like mist or a distant cloud which cannot be distinguished from the sky. Hence, except at the opening in the envelope of compressed air, we see neither the fire in the hollow wheel, nor the wheel itself, just as the sky behind mist or cloud is invisible to us. The movement of the sun across the heaven is simply the displacement of the opening due to the wheel's revolution. These two models—the revolving wheels and the fire appearing at the mouth of the forge—are perfect examples of technical analogy. . . . The use of the mechanical analogy . . . [is part of] the picture of the scientific approach which distinguished Ancient Greece from all that went before. (Pp. 13-15).

We arrive, finally, at a contribution of Anaximander's that deserves especial stress: his conception of the processes of cosmic formation and dissolution. Even Thales had done no more than to seek an *Urstoff*, and this is yet a far cry from Anaximander's effort to describe the natural development of our orderly cosmos out of something that could plausibly be conceived as the primordial, unordered condition of the universe. His attempt to provide a comprehensive description of the evolution of our cosmos as resulting from the natural working-out of physical processes mark Anaximander as the founder of scientific cosmogony. As such, he inaugurates a strain of inquiry which, after a brief and abortive history in early Greek thought lay dormant until the days of Kant and Laplace.

For such reasons as these, it is clear that—despite the fact that only a few scraps of his original writings have come down to us (and this largely by dint of their imaginative qualities!)—Anaximander deserves an important place in the history of scientific thought. If modern reconstructions of his teachings have any merit, it is indefensible to deny Anaximander recognition as one of the earliest workers within the truest tradition of the scientific endeavor to understand the world about us wholly from the standpoint of the operation of natural processes.

But even apart from his contributions to science, Anaximander deserves an outstanding place in the intellectual history of the race. Since the most primitive times, men have been awed and impressed by the contrast between the transient phenomena of earthly life on the one hand and on the other the seemingly unchanging regularity of the heavens. Man's life is short, and lived but once, while the heavens appear eternal and the movements of the celestial orbs exhibits a marvellous cyclic constancy. This contrast has ever inspired so profound and awesome sentiments that these have constantly intruded themselves into religion, beginning in even the earliest times, and lasting far past the days of Anaximander. To conceive of even the celestial order as temporary and transitory—to deem the whole history of our universe as a transient thing, natural evolutionary processes having brought into being a cosmos that has no more permanence in the vast reaches of the "order of time" than does the span of a generation in the life of mankind—this is a break with even the highest modes of primitive thought that is of astonishing magnitude. This achievement of Anaximander's is surely one that speaks of an intellect of truly amazing grasp and audacity.[28]

NOTES

1   References of this type are to the section on Anaximander in Diels-Kranz, *Die Fragmente der Vorsokratiker* (6th ed., Berlin, 1951). The letter refers to the subsection, the number *before* the decimal point to the paragraph number given by Diels-Kranz. In the event that several items are given in the paragraph, the appropriate number of the item in question (first, second, third, etc.) is indicated *after* the decimal point. Wherever possible, I have used either the translation in the Loeb Classical Library series, or that of A. Fairbanks, *The First Philosophers of Greece* (London, 1898).

2   See the discussion of this point in G.S. Kirk, "Some Problems in Anaximander," *Classical Quarterly*, vol. 48 (1955), pp. 21-28.

3   Simplicius here speaks in terms of Aristotle's conception of the *apeiron* as a material thing (*apeiron soma*) (A 16.4).

4   I do not of course urge that Anaximander explicitly entertained these two alternatives and made a deliberate choice between them, but merely that is was boundlessness, and not literal infinitude, that he had in mind with regard to the spatial extension of the *apeiron*.

5   These ideas will be elaborated in detail below.

6   This functional duality of the *apeiron* led Diels to translate the term into German as "das grenzenlos-Unbestimmbare." (*Fragmente der Vorsokratiker*, p. 89.)

7   R. Mondolfo ("Problemi della cosmologia d'Anassimandro," *Logos*, vol. 20 [1937], pp. 14-30) endorses (pp. 18-19) the view of A. Rey (*La jeunesse de la science grècque* [Paris, 1933], pp. 75 ff.) that Anaximander's *apeiron* is to be conceived of on the lines of the chaos depicted by Plato in the *Timaeus*. I agree that Plato's discussion of the Receptacle and its original condition is strongly influenced by Anaximandrean ideas:

"Only in speaking of that *in* which all of them [the elements] are always coming to be, making their appearance and again vanishing out of it, may we use the words 'this' of 'that'; we must not apply any of these words to that which is of some quality—hot or cold or any of the opposites—or to any combination of these opposites . . . [But it] must be said of that nature which receives all bodies [that] it must be called always the same; for since it never departs at all from its own character; since it is always receiving all things, and never in any way whatsoever takes on any character that is like any of the things that enter it. By nature it is there as a matrix for everything . . . . For this reason, then, the mother and

Receptacle of what has come to be visible and otherwise sensible must not be called earth or air or fire or water, nor any of their compounds or components; but we shall not be deceived if we call it a nature invisible and characterless, all-receiving, partaking in some very puzzling way of the intelligible and very hard to apprehend . . .[The Receptacle] is Space, which is everlasting, not admitting of destruction; providing a situation for all things that come into being, but itself apprehended without the senses by a sort of bastard reasoning . . . [At the beginning of cosmic development, the matrix] had every sort of diverse appearance to the sight; but because it was filled with powers that were neither alike nor evenly balanced, there was no equipoise in any region of it; but it was everywhere swayed unevenly and shaken by these things [i.e., its constituents], and by its motion shook them in turn.   And they, being thus moved, were perpetually being separated and carried in different directions . . . Before that [i.e., the separation of the distinct elements], all these kinds were without proportion or measure" (49 B-53 B. Adapted from Cornford's translation in *Plato's Cosmology* [London, 1937], pp. 179-198).

This discussion of Plato's seems to be much influenced by Anaximander's book so far as the fundamental ideas are concerned; their *articulation* is, of course, bound up with conceptions subsequent to Anaximander.

[8]   This suggests that Anaximander conceived of his *original flooding* of the world (Alexander, A 27.2, and see below) along the lines of a dew at the "dawn of history."

[9]   See Hippolytus, A 11; Aristotle, A 16.2; Aetios, A 18, A 21.1, A 21.3, A 21.4, A 23.1, A 24, A 27.3, A 29, A 30.1; Achilles, A 21.1; Seneca, A 23.2; Alexander, A 27.2; and Ammian, A 28.

[10]   Since the foregoing discussion of the *apeiron* preceded consideration of Anaximander's concept of process, the vaporous nature of the *apeiron*, strongly suggested by the latter, was not brought out explicitly. It was clearly apprehended by Aristotle, who writes that the *apeiron* is "something denser than fire and rarer than air" (A 16.2). P. Tannery writes: "Upon careful examination of his doctrine, no doubt whatever can remain that Anaximander had in mind a very specific conception of the *apeiron*, and this, it would seem, must have been as an air-like fluid, composed of water vapor . . . Anaximenes had merely to preserve his teachings in this matter." *Science hellène* (3d edition, Paris, 1930), p. 104.

[11]   Here I adopt the thesis of W.A. Heidel and of J. Burnet (See Burnet, EGP, pp. 61-62) that the idea of a cosmic *dinê* is basic to the cosmogony of Anaximander. Burnet rightly insists that the *eternal motion, qua* the primordial motion present in the apeiron, is not a *dinê*, which comes to be only in the formation of the cosmos.

Aristotle tells us (A 15) that the *apeiron* "surrounds all things and steers all" (*kai periechein hapanta kai panta kybernan*). (This is probably a direct quotation. See G.S. Kirk and J.E. Raven, *The Presocratic Philosophers* [Cambridge, 1957], pp. 114-115.) This description accords well with the formation of the cosmos from an eddy *within the apeiron* (cf. *ibid.*, pp. 128-29).

12   That is, the center of the world. "Anaximander says that the earth is a celestial object (*meteôros*) and is positioned in the center of the cosmos" (Theon of Smyrna, A 26.2).

13   As already remarked above, this passage embodies Anaximandrian elements of thought.

14   S. Sambursky in his book on *The Physical World of the Greeks* (London, 1956) provides an illuminating commentary on this conception:

[According to Anaximander] the creation of the world began when a certain portion of this formless mass [the *apeiron*] was detached from the rest, thus setting in motion a process of differentiation which produced the beginnings of order by separating out the two opposed qualities, hot and cold. The significance of this separation is twofold. First of all it means, in the terminology of modern physics, that every physical occurrence in the cosmos can only come about through the existence of a difference in potentials which makes a transition from one level to another possible, e.g., thermic differences, differences in the gravitational or electric potential, etc. For this reason, the task of every cosmogony, from Anaximander to the present day, is to explain how such gradients come about in a homogeneous environment which does not contain them. Secondly, as regards the particular case of the specific contrast picked on by Anaximander, our cosmos displays the special separation of cold which is located on the earth, from hot which is found in the heavens: the way in which this division came into being also calls for a physical explanation. (Pp. 185-86.)

15   These reports of Hippolytus and Aristotle on the enternality of the *apeiron* yield us two of our very few (five in all) direct quotes from the writings of Anaximander (see B 2 and B 3).

16   I fully accept the view of F.M. Cornford that "Anaximander held that his infinite stuff existed in its undifferentiated state *outside* our world, which it envelops" (Aristotle's *Physics*, Loeb, vol. I, p. 234, notes).

17   It is only in this sense, as a ring *split off* from the "fire around the world" that it is correct to say (as Diogenes Laertius misleadingly does) that Anaximander taught that the moon shines "with borrowed light and derives its illumination from the sun" (A 1).

[18] See also Aristotle, A 26.1, and compare Plato, *Phaedo*, 118 E, and Origen, *Philosophoumena*, c. 6.

[19] Thus if 3 is used as value of π, the ratio of the height of the earth cylinder to its circumference is 1:9. This ratio plays a very important role in the cosmology of Anaximander, as we shall see below.

[20] The thesis attributed to Anaximander by Aetios that "the sun is equal in size to the earth" (A 21.3) must be interpreted as asserting that the size of this weak spot is the same as the size of the face of the earth.

[21] This matter was first clarified by H. Diels, "Über Anaximandros' Kosmos," *Archiv für Geschichte der Philosophie*, vol. 10 (1879), pp. 228.ff.

[22] See Burnet, EGP, p. 68; and also P. Tannery, *Science hellène*, [2d ed., Paris, 1930], p. 91, and H. Diels, "Über Anaximandros' Kosmos."

[23] Anaximander is credited with the introduction into Greece of the *gnomon*, an upright rod the motion of whose shadow with the movement of the sun is used for timekeeping, i.e., a sundial (Diogenes, A 1; Suidas, A 2; Eusebius, A 4). Observations made by means of this device no doubt provided the basis for Anaximander's conception of the movement of sunlight over the earth's surface.

[24] These considerations lead P. Tannery to discuss Anaximander's view in the light of the modern physical concept of *entropy*. (*Science hellène*, pp. 109-18.)

[25] It has been a matter of controversy if Anaximander's "innumerable worlds" are *simultaneous* (as with the Eleatic atomists) or *successive*, Burnet (EGP, p. 58) has argued against Zeller (*Philosophie der Griechen*, rev. by W. Nestle [7th ed., Leipzig, 1923], pp. 310 ff.) that the plurality of worlds is contemporaneous rather than successive. F. Cornford (*Classical Quarterly*, vol. 28 [1934], pp. 1-16) has surveyed all the evidence that has been brought to bear on both sides of the argument, and has shown, in a way that is to my mind highly persuasive, that it is Zeller's view that the "innumerable worlds" are *successive* that must be adopted. I here adopt this view. It must be said to depend in the last analysis on the question if the *apeiron* is strictly infinite or merely boundless, and on my reading of Anaximander's thought the second is the more likely.

This cyclic aspect of Anaximander's cosmology, it should also be remarked, renders otiose Aristotle's suggestion that Anaximander viewed the *archê* as infinite because he thought that "from the unfailing persistence of genesis . . . it follows that the things which come into being are drawn from an unlimited store" (A 15; cf. *idem* A 143, Simplicius A 17.2, and Aetios A 14.1). This misunderstanding of Aristotle's persists in his school, because they follow him (see e.g., Aetios A 14.2) in insisting upon viewing the *apeiron* as a material substratum that is *used* up in the cycle of coming to be and passing away.

[26]   To my mind, S. Sambursky has come far closer to he mark in characterizing the nature of the concept of *apeiron*: "Anaximander did not think fit to give the primordial matter a name, since any specification would necessarily have deprived it of the essential characteristic which was the reason for its conception: namely, its complete lack of attributes. Anaximander's words show us how his opinions are to be understood. He saw that the cyclical changes of nature bring into being and destroy certain opposed qualities. . . . None of the opposites can achieve absolute domination and annihilate the others. In this respect they are all limited, i.e., finite in place and time. But they are all products of the unlimited primordial matter. . . . This unlimited substance is not only devoid of any specific qualities but is also the substratum of all physical phenomena and their mutations. In the language of modern science we should say that it is the origin of all the physical quantities, whether mass or energy in all its forms, whether electric charge or nuclear and gravitational forces. In the words of one of the later commentators: 'He found the origin of things not in the change of matter, but in the separation of the opposites (from the unlimited) by means of an unending motion' (Simplicius, A 9). these separated opposites are the physical qualities which can be physically defined and which, being specific, are therefore limited. The unlimited, on the contrary, is the ultimate entity, unanalysable and indivisible: any attempt to give it a specific name or mark of identification transposes it into the world of specific concepts." (*The Physical World of the Greeks* [London, 1956], pp. 8-9.)

[27]   *A History of Science: Ancient Science Through the Golden Age of Greece* (Cambridge, Mass., 1952), pp. 175-77.

[28]   [Added in 2005.] This essay was originally published in *Studium Generale*, vol. 12 (1959), pp. 718-731. It thus antedated Charles H. Kahn's excellent book on *Anaximander and the Origins of Greek Cosmology* (New York, 1960), whose discussion, however, provides no ground for any revisions. A highly instructive more recent treatment is Robert Hahn, *Anaximander and the Architects* (Albany, NY: State University of New York Press, 2001). And see also D. L. Cauprie, Robert Hahn, and Geril Naddaf, *Anaximander in Context* (Albany, NY: State University of New York Press, 2003).

Chapter 2

CONTRASTIVE OPPOSITION IN EARLY GREEK PHILOSOPHY

1. INTRODUCTION

The history of Greek philosophy in its earlier stages is often presented in the manner of a Cook's tour: now here, now there: today, Anaximander with his *apeiron*; tomorrow, Heraclitus with his flowing river; day after, Pythagoras with his numerology. But what is actually at issue here is in many respects an orderly and coherent development that unfolds an evolving idea through coherent series of sequential stages.

As the ancients themselves in fact saw it, by taking the path of a thematically issue-oriented (doxographic) unfolding rather than personalistically thinker-oriented (biographic) approach, one is able to get a clearer and in some respects more instructive view of the development of philosophical thought. The aim of the present discussion is to offer an instructive illustration of this phenomenon, namely the evolution of the doctrine of contrastive opposition. Accordingly, the motivating thesis of this discussion is that a significant sector of early Greek philosophy can be depicted in terms of the development and elaboration of the theory of opposites.

2. ELEMENTS AND OPPOSITES

Thought about nature (*physis*) among the early Greeks—their philosophy of nature, if that is not too grandiose an expression to describe it—was based on the idea of "the four elements": air, earth, fire, and water. And these were seen as characterized in terms of two fundamental descriptive contrasts wet/dry and hot/cold in the following manner:

	wet	*dry*
hot	AIR	FIRE
cold	WATER	EARTH

In this manner, early Greek theorizing about physical reality was based on the combinatorial machinations of two fundamental physically operative opposites—hot/cold and wet/dry—whose machinations were seen as explaining the nature and function of four basic elements.

These primitive, pre-philosophical ideas of elements and opposites were to play an important ongoing role in the development of Greek philosophical thought. The present discussion will illustrate this with respect to the latter: the conception of opposites (*enantia*).

3. PROLIFERATING AND ARITHMETIZING OPPOSITES: PYTHAGORAS (ca. 570 - ca. 497)

Building on the foundation of the rudimentary elements and opposites, Pythagoras and his school devised a complex and sophisticated theory of opposites predicated on four principal ideas: a proliferation of opposites far beyond the two elemental pairs; a factorial linkage of opposites; a quantification of opposites as matters of degree; and a harmonization of opposites in varying proportions. Let us briefly consider each in turn.

Proliferation. The Pythagoreans envisioned a substantial plurality of opposites, including not only hot/cold and wet/dry but also: small/large, light/heavy, young/old, dark/light, and many others. Accordingly, nature as Pythagoras saw it, pivots not on that single pair of fundamental opposites but on a vast proliferation of opposing types.

Factorial linkage. The Pythagorean approach to opposites further involved the idea that the opposites are always connected in that they involve a slide along the scale of a single descriptive factor ("parameter" we would call it) that connects these opposing extremes as per:

- *moistness* in the case of dry/wet
- *size* in the case of small/large
- *weight* in the case of light/heavy
- *age* in the case of young/old
- *temperature* in the case of cold/hot

Each of those opposition-contrasts is thus conjoined along the sliding scale of a parametric factor whose increase/decrease links these opposites together. In each case there is a difference of extent with respect to a linking factor that unites those factors in a thematic unity.

Quantification. Pythagoras and his school proceeded to extend this coordinative conjunction from the merely comparative idea of more or less to the idea of an actually quantitative measurement. They sought to quantify and indeed arithmetize the matter of opposition, moving from a mere comparison of extent to a measure (*metron*) that is specifiable by ratios. Thus consider

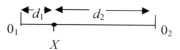

Here the ratio d_1: d_2 serves to specify a particular position in this opposite-range 0_1-to-0_2.

And so, if one contemplates an ontology where different natural types are defined by their varying placement in a spectrum of opposition ranges, then it makes perfect sense to claim that different sorts of things are defined, (determined, specified) by numbers, that is by ratios with respect to a spectrum of opposites.

Such an approach clearly opens the way to a vastly enriched view of nature—in particular once matters of degree are contemplated. Thus even if for each opposite pair we contemplate just five states with respect to degree or extent as per

very $+\vert$ somewhat $+\vert$ neutral $\vert$ somewhat $-\vert$ very $-$

then with just eight opposite pairs we will have $5 \times 5 \times 5 \times 5 \times 5 \times 5 \times 5 \times 5 = 5^8 = 390{,}625$) state-descriptive combinations. Nature now takes on a vastly diversified—and decidedly more realistic—complexity.

Harmonization. From quantification, the Pythagoreans moved on to the idea that even as only certain ratios are sufficiently "harmonious" to characterize sounds in music, so only certain ratios are sufficiently "harmonious" to characterize types of objects in nature. On this basis, the Pythagoreans elaborated the theory of natural opposites with the ideas of ratios, proportions, and harmonies to give a mathematical cast to the theory.

Moreover, the Pythagoreans extended their approach from physics to psychology. Building on the doctrine of the four elements, Greek medicine had distinguished four kinds of moisture—of fluids, as it were—in the human body:

dominant element	*bodily fluid* ("humor")
fire	choler (yellow bile)
air	melancholy (black bile)
water	blood
earth	phlegm

A complex theory of bodily health was built on the issue of a proper balancing among these four bodily humors, as well as a theory of personality-types geared to the issue of what humor predominated in the overall mixture.[1]

By meshing this doctrine of element-domination in bodily fluids with their theory of opposites, the Pythagorean school elaborated a bio-medical theory in which proportion, balance, blending, and harmonization also figured prominently in matters of diet and the maintenance of health. On this basis, Pythagorean doctrine became intertwined with the medical theories of Hippocrates (b. ca. 460) in whose wake Greek medicine contemplated two alternative pathways to the pathology of balance restoration: one, allopathy, calling for redressing balance by an opposite medicament and the other, homeopathy, reducing balance by additional small doses of the same opposite in the expectation of providing a counter-reaction.

4. RELATIVIZING OPPOSITES: XENOPHANES OF COLOPHON (ca. 570 - ca. 480)

Xenophanes was, so Aristotle tells us, the first to insist upon the fundamental unity of things.[2] He took a decidedly original view of the opposites. For him the opposites such as sweet/bitter are not facets of nature or reality, but merely represent how things seem to us humans. As Xenophanes saw it, if honey did not exist, men would deem figs to be the paradigm of sweetness.[3] For Xenophanes, the oppositions which his predecessors saw as constitutive of nature are actually no more than artifacts of human response. On this basis, Xenophanes held a relativistic, and contextualistic view of the opposites as an anthropomorphic epiphenomenon in the setting of a fundamentally unified nature.

5. NORMATIVIZING OPPOSITES: HERACLITUS (ca. 540 - ca. 480?)

With the Pythagoreans, Heraclitus stressed the multiplicity of opposites. And in this light, Heraclitus made the following principal points regarding opposites:

1. There are many of them. And in general they relate to the reactivity of organisms: animal or (principally) human. Health/illness, light/dark, waking/sleeping, war/peace.

2. They are generally evaluative, with one side good one bad, as per: health/illness, satiety/hunger, rest/tiredness, satisfaction/unpleasantness.

3. Whether something is good or bad does not depend simply on its own particular character, but on the nature of the interagent. Thus drinking sea water is injurious to men but healthful to fish; mud-wallowing is unpleasant to men but delightful to pigs; swill is pleasant to donkeys but unpleasant to men (and inversely for gold); etc. One selfsame item will make an opposite impact on different recipients.

For Heraclitus the most salient opposites are not the physical—whose operations in nature he deemed beset by instability—but the evaluative (axiological, affective), along the spectrum of good/bad, harmful/salutary, positive/negative, right/wrong. Heraclitus thus insists that opposition in the value spectrum does not lie in the object itself but arises relationally in the responses they woke. Things in and of themselves are neutral, indifferent until an interactive response engenders their positivity or negativity one way or the other. Reactivity apart, matters remain in a unity of indifference. In this way those evaluative opposites are not intrinsic but evocative, not absolute and inherent in things themselves, but reagent-relative through interactive engenderment. All depending on conditions and circumstances, there exists in one selfsame being both life and death, waking and sleeping, youth and old age.[4]

Moreover, the role of tension and conflict is crucial. In and of itself the string of the lyre is soundless; it is solely through the tension of opposed impetuses that it is able to produce a pleasing sound. Thus the Pythagorean

thesis of measure, ratio, proportion, and balance also represents a key feature in the thought of Heraclitus.[5] However, he responded to the Pythagorean proliferation of opposites by adding two important ideas: That what
matters with opposites is not so much *balance* as *tension* between opposing
forces, and that the defining factors for opposites are not intrinsic but reac-
tive/dispositional. As Heraclitus saw it, Anaxagoras was wrong in stressing
the inherent features of opposites and Pythagoras was wrong in emphasiz-
ing balance and harmony instead of tension and divergence.

6. PARTITIONING (AND MIXING) OPPOSITES: ANAXAGORAS (ca. 500 - 428)

For Anaxagoras there is one single basic basis of *material* being—as opposed to mind (*nous*)—a "stuff" (as one might call it) that contains everything mixed up together. But with portions of this stuff as "seeds" these
arise through separate different proportions of the constituents. In this way
there comes to be a separating out through which there emerge material
kinds differentiated by then characteristic proportions of exactly the same
ingredients, pretty much as per the Pythagorean picture:

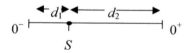

Thus for any type of opposition 0, any type of substance S has a typical
S-determinative position along the 0^- to 0^+ spectrum, say at the indicated
division $d_1:d_2$. On this basis, the ratio $\frac{d_1}{d_1+d_2}$ defines the 0-status (the "extent
of 0-ness," if you please) that a unit quantity of the substance S has. Overall, the composition of the substance will be defined by a characteristic
mode of the basic stuff there is, which contains a bit of everything there is
altogether.
     But of course if everything is composed of the same oppositional "in-
gredients," then the net effect is that everything is mixed up, as it were, so
that the composition of anything would pretty much encompass something
of everything else.   Such a line of thought leads straightaway to the

Anaxagorean concept of mixture (*symmixis*). For on this basis we can see that every type of substance there is will contain some (generally very small) amounts of every other type of thing that there is.

Following in the footsteps of Anaximander, Anaxagoras also envisioned a theory of cosmic evolution. Initially there was a chaos, a tohu-bohu in which all of those descriptive oppositions were thoroughly intermingled with one another but gradually mind/nous separated out units of different things determined as such by their appropriate proportion. In this manner Anaxagoreans, like the Pythagoreans, saw reason and proportion, in the dual sense of *logos* (*ratio*), as a constituting force operative within the natural world.

7. EMPEDOCLES (ca. 495 - ca. 435)

Some of the other salient theses of his predecessors also recur in starring roles in the philosophy of Empedocles. For him the four elements (now called "roots": *horizômata*) are basic and their mixture through a process of separation and union under the aegis of the cosmic force of love and strife leads to the birth and death of the world's constituents. But in opposition to the response-relativity of Xenophanes, Empedocles reverts to the more substantive conception of the opposites as found in the earlier teaching of Milesian nature philosophy. In this regard—as in his looking back to the ideas of Hesiod—Empedocles chose to swim against the currents of his time by looking back to the tendencies of earlier thinking.

8. PLATO (427 - 347)

In the *Philebus*, Plato set out a general account—effectively a *theory*—of opposites. Its main points are these:

1. Some opposites are limitless (*apeiron*), for example, hot/cold. There can always be something yet hotter than something that is hot, and similarly with cold. Such opposites are always a matter of more or less with such pluralization as very little/slightly/some-what/decidedly/ very much as per: very cold/cold/tepid/hot/very hot which in turn can be perfected yet further. (*Philebus* 24a-25a.) Effectively all of the physical opposites are of this nature: dry/wet, high/low, quick/slow, greater/ smaller. (*Philebus*, 25c.) In this regard—

2. For all of the opposites that are matter of degree of some common factor, there is a shared "ground" or "cause" (*aitia*)—a factor whose presence as more or less accounts for the opposites:

> weight: heavier/lighter
> size: larger/smaller
> age: older/younger
> moisture: wetter/drier
> height: higher/lower
> and the like

3. Some opposites have a limit on one side or the other (or both). Plato gives no examples but seems to have in mind such examples as straight/curved for lines (with one limit) or odd/even for integers (with two), or same/different, or equal/unequal. (*Philebus*, 25a). Moreover—

4. Some opposites are mixable in nature: they allow of blending or combination (*mixis*) and others do not. For example, hot/cold is a mixture-admitting operation: The very hot can combine with—and cancel out—the very cold to yield what is merely tepid. Or again consider half/double. The half of a number mixed with the double to yield the same. (*Philebus*, 25a-b.) But the straight does not mix with the crooked to yield something intermediate, nor the odd with the even.

However, Plato's principal innovation lay in shifting the consideration of opposites into an inquiry into the good for man. In the *Philebus* (20c - 22c), Socrates and his interlocutor deliberate about the nature of what is good in life and the good life as such and the deliberations set out here effectively transmuted the Pythagorean-Heracleitean concept of opposition in relation to bio-medical balance of physical health to their application in matters of spirited health in relation to the good life and the good of life. The net effect shift from the bio-medical to the psychological, from the mere reactivity of Xenophanes and Heraclitus to the constitution of human character.

9. ARISTOTLE (384 - 322)

We find an important elaboration of opposition in Aristotle's doctrine of the logical opposition in *De Interpretatione* where the conception of logical contraries and contradictories stands in the foreground. The former exemplified by such instances as all/none, or great/small wherever there is a "middle ground" between the opposites. And the latter is exemplified by such instances as some/none or (in the case of integers) odd/even. In Aristotle's logic (analytics), seen as the theory of rational demonstration, the concept of opposition plays a prominent and far-reaching part.[6]

In developing the theory of opposites as such, Aristotle begins by focusing on the logico-linguistic aspects of the matter, and accordingly distinguishes four modes of opposition:[7]

1. *Opposition by relation* (*pros ti*). Examples: more/less, double/half)

2. *Opposition by contrariety* (*enantia*). Examples: black/white, odd/even, good/bad, hot/cold.

3. *Opposition by privation* (*kata sterêsin kai hexin*). Examples: sight/blindness, hearing/deafness, wisdom/folly.

4. *Opposition by contradiction* (*kat' antiphrasin*). Examples: just/unjust, virtuous/vicious, beautiful/ugly.

Those responsive reaction oppositions at issue with human excellence all seem to fall into that third category. In each case a proper and appropriate something is called for in a way that positions the sagacious *phronimos* intermediately undecidedly between the two extremes of too little and too much.

At this point we arrive at the Aristotelian doctrine of the mean was designed to address the question of human excellence. The basic idea, in brief compass, is that it is moral excellence (*ethike arête*), which, in turn is a settled state (*hexis*) that is, as he puts it "concerned with choice (*prohairesis*) in the mean (*mesotês*) that is relative to us humans and is rationally determined as a truly wise man (*phronimos*) would determine it"[8]. But just what sort of us-relative mean is at issue here?

As Aristotle saw it, the demand of reason and wisdom is a matter of "a sense of proportion"—of keeping one's balance by clearing to the sensible position between extremes of too little and too much—to strive for the reflectively warranted intermediate position between extremes: the appropriate means. It is a matter of keeping one's actions and reactions geared to the proper intermediation where such all-too-human emotions as anger, fear, pity, self-confidence, gratitude and the like come into play. Thus when insulted it is appropriate to be high on the anger side, low on the gratitude side; when placed in a digression situation a variable degree of fear is in order, as is a reasonable degree of confidence.

Excellence, as Aristotle saw it, is a state of character based on moderation: it is a disposition towards realizing an intermediate mean between having "too much of a good thing" (as the colloquial expression has it) and having too little. Appropriate intermediacy looks to a mean (*mesotês*) positioned between two defects (*kakiai*), those of deficiency and excess. Manifest examples of Aristotelian intermediations are:

- proper indignation as a mean between pusillanimous impatience, unconcern, and uncontrolled fury.

- due respect as a mean between callous indifference and fawning.

- due heed as a mean between mindless neglect and hyperpreoccupation.

Even as the eye cannot see properly where there is too little light or too much or as the body cannot function properly when one eats too much or too little, so someone is in trouble who has too much self-esteem (the egocentrist) or too little (the self indifferent).

Thus where the Pythagoreans had approached opposite-harmonization in the context of *physical* health and Plato had seen it in the context of *psychological* health, Aristotle stressed its being in the context of *ethical* health. The focus here is less upon the *psyche* than upon the *daimon* (*eudemonia*), and the wise man is one who judges appropriately just what is called for across the spectrum of circumstances.

Aristotle's doctrine of the mean thus combines in an integrative synthesis the oppositional pluralism of Anaxagoras, the harmonious balance and proportionality of Pythagoreans, the humanly geared axiology of Heraclitus, and the oppositional pychologism of Plato into a complex theory of human excellence. Accordingly, the Aristotelian doctrine of the Golden Mean can and should be seen as the ethical culmination of a course of conceptual evolution setting out from the physico-ontological theory of opposites of the earlier pre-Socratic philosophers.

10. SUMMARY

As our survey indicates, the principal steps in the evolution of the theory of contrastive opposites in early Greek philosophy are registered in the following sequence.

* The four physical elements and two natural opposites of early Greek pre-philosophical cosmology.

* The multiple natural opposites of the Pythagoreans and the ideas of mixture and mathematical harmonization among them.

* The medicalization of opposition in the humoral theory of Hippocratic medicine.

* The biologicization of Heraclitus and his doctrine of tensions and balancings.

* The doctrine human reactivity with its anthropocentric shift as articulated by Xenophanes.

* The Anaxagorean idea of *mixture*: of pervasive compositeness in relation to physical being.

* The Platonic shift of the Pythagoreans idea of tension and mixture from the medical (bio-physical) domain to that of spiritual health with its transition from the stress on physical health in Pythagoras and Heraclitus to the condition of the health spirit (*psyche*) as balanced.

* The Aristotelian shift from psychic well-being to ethical goodness with his theory of the golden mean shifting the issue from that of psychic well being (eupsychim) to ethical well being (eudaimonism).

And so, the idea of opposites and their machinations traces out a continuous line of issue-geared development across the spectrum of doctrinally diverse thinkers who constitute the history of early Greek philosophy. For there is, in fact, a stepwise-evolving series of stages leading from the pre-philosophical Greek cosmology of opposites to Aristotle's doctrine of the golden mean. Accordingly, the history of opposites in their journey from the role of opposition *in nature* to its role in relation to *the human good*—first in its psychological and then in its spiritual dimension—both parallels and typifies the transit of early Greek philosophizing from a an exclusive focus on processes of nature to one preoccupied with wisdom regarding the conduct of life.

The salient point here is that the theory of opposites affords an instructive illustration as a case study in the development of early Greek thought as a natural unfolding of certain key ideas through substantively interconnected stages. What this journey represents is a coherent process of evolution via a succession of cogent responses to developed positions. There is little question but that the development of this sector of philosophical history traces out an orderly path rather than a random walk, constituting a course of development that is decidedly dialectical, albeit by way of *inviting* certain responses rather than (as per Hegel) *demanding* them through the inherent logic of the situation. In this regard the situation is that of a dialectic that seizes upon thematic opportunities rather than being a Hegelian dialectic of logico-historical necessitation.

NOTES

[1] For an entrée into the extensive literature on humoral theory in Geek medicine see the bibliography in James Longrigg, *Greek Medicine* (New York: Routledge, 1998). See also Vivian Nutton, *Ancient Medicine* (London: Routledge, 2004), especially pp. 121-22.

[2] *Metaphysics*, A5, 986b21.

[3] Frag. 189, KRS p. 179. (Here KRS abbreviates G. S. Kirk, J. E. Raven and M. Schofield, *The Presocratic Philosophers*, 2nd. ed. (Cambridge: Cambridge University Press 1983).

[4] KRS, p. 189, frag. 209.

[5] See KRS, pp. 197-98.

[6] For an instructive discussion of the relevant issues see C. W. A. Whitaker, *Aristotle's De interpretatione: Contradiction and Dialectic* (Oxford: Clarendon Press, 1996).

[7] The relevant passages include: *Categories*, X; 11b15-13b35; *Topics*, II, 109b18-35 and 113b1-15; *Metaphysics*, passim; *On Interpretation*, IV, 17a37-18a13; *Prior Analytics*, II, 63b21-64b2.

[8] *Nichomachen Ethics*, 1106b36.

Chapter 3

THOUGHT EXPERIMENTATION IN PRESOCRATIC PHILOSOPHY

1. INTRODUCTION: THOUGHT EXPERIMENTS

In intellectual regards, *homo sapiens* is an amphibian who lives and functions in two very different realms—the domain of existing reality that we can investigate in observational inquiry, and the domain of imaginative projection that we can explore in thought through reasoning. And this second ability becomes crucially important for the first as well, when once one presses beyond the level of a mere *description* of the real to concern ourselves also with its rational *explanation*, which involves providing for an account of why things are as they are rather than otherwise. In the history of Western thought this transition was first made, as far as we can tell, by the Greek nature-philosophers of Presocratic times. It is they who invented thought-experimentation as a cognitive procedure and—as will be seen—practiced it with considerable dedication and versatility.

A "thought experiment" is an attempt to draw instruction from a process of hypothetical reasoning that proceeds by eliciting the consequences of an hypothesis which, for aught that one actually knows to the contrary, may well be false. It consists in reasoning from a supposition that is not (or not yet) accepted as true—and perhaps is even known to be false—but is assumed provisionally in the interests of making a point or establishing a conclusion.[1]

In natural science, thought experiments are common. Think, for example, of Abert Einstein's pondering the question of what the world would look like if one were to travel along a ray of light. Think too of the physicists' assumption of a frictionlessly rolling body or the economists' assumption of a perfectly efficient market in the interests of establishing the laws of descent or the principles of exchange, respectively. Indeed thought experiments are far more common in science than one may think. For Ernest Mach made the sound point that any sensibly designed *real* experiment should be preceded by a *thought* experiment that anticipates at any rate the possibility of its outcome.[2]   The conclusion of *such* a thought experiment will clearly be hypothetical: "If the experiment turns out X-wise, we shall be in a position to conclude ...." There is thus good reason to see thought experimentation as an indispensably useful accompaniment to actual experimentation.[3]

To us moderns, brought up on imaginative childrens' nursery rhymes ("If wishes were horses, then beggars would ride") and accustomed to obvious adult fictions, this sort of belief-suspensive thinking seems altogether natural.   It takes a logician to appreciate how complex and sophisticated thought experimentation actually is.   For what it involves is *not* simply the drawing of an appropriate conclusion from a given fact, but also the higher-level consideration that a particular thesis (be it fact or mere supposition) carries a certain conclusion in its wake.

It is thus interesting to note that the use of thought experimentation in philosophy is as old as the subject itself.   For, as this brief discussion will endeavor to substantiate, it was already a prominent instrumentality in the thought of the Presocratic nature-philosophers of ancient Greece who launched the philosophical enterprise on its way.   The present discussion is, accordingly, a small contribution towards that yet nonexistent (or at any rate greatly undeveloped) discipline, the history of modes of argumentation and reasoning.

2. THALES OF MILETUS

Thought experimentation is *explanatory* in character when it inheres in a line of reasoning of the form: "X is hard to account for, but if we assume that P, which we certainly don't know but which is not inherently implausible, then we obtain a perfectly good explanation of X." This projection of a conjectural reason in the interests of explanatory understanding represents a perfectly sensible use of thought experimentation, and actually affords its very oldest use in the philosophical domain.   For this sort of explanatory use of thought experimentation was already used by Thales of Miletus (b. ca. 620 B.C.), the first of these Presocratic nature philosophers. As we learn from Aristotle and his followers:

> [Thales held that the flooding of the Nile occurs because] "the Elesian winds, blowing straight on to Egypt, raise up the mass of the Nile's water through cutting off its outflow by the swelling of the sea coming against it." (Aetius IV, 1, a; Kirk & Raven, p. 77.)[4]

[Thales taught] "that the earth floats on the water, and that it stays in place though floating like a log or some other such thing …" (Aristotle, *De Caelo*, B13, 294a28; Kirk & Raven, p. 87.)

[Thales and Hippon] Declared it [the *psyche*] to be made of water, apparently being persuaded by considering seeds, which are all moist. (Aristotle, *De Anima*, A 2, 405 bl; Kirk & Raven, p. 90.)

This sort of use of thought experimentation in the context of explanatory conjectures answers to the following pattern:

METHOD NO. 1 (Explanatory Conjectures)

- It is to be shown that *P* is the case (where it has not yet been established whether *P* or not-*P*).

- Assume—as "thought experiment"—that *P* is the case (which is not inherently implausible).

- Explain *Q* on the basis of this assumption, where *Q* is something patently true which we could not readily explain otherwise.

- Hence maintain that *P*.

The reasoning attributed to Thales throughout the preceding examples illustrates exactly this pattern of thought. Take the case of the position of the earth as a body that remains fixed on its place under the canopy of the heavens:

- To show: the earth floats on water (like a log).

- Assume this to be so, that is, suppose that the earth floats (like a log) on a large body of water.

- Note that this supposition will naturally explain the earth's remaining in its place in nature (and does so at least as well as any available alternative).

- Therefore: we are justified in claiming that the earth floats on water (like a log).

Again, consider the case of the *psyche*, the principle of life, regarded as that which enables living things to be living, and which all living things thus have to have in common. Here we have:

- To show: that the *psyche* is made of water.

- Assume this to be so, that is, suppose that the *psyche* is made of water naturally explains why all seeds both have moistness in them and need water to develop.

- Note that this supposition that the *psyche* is made of water naturally explains why all seeds both have moistness in them and need water to develop.

- Therefore: we are justified in claiming that the *psyche* is made of water.

The Elesian winds case can also clearly be accommodated by the same overall pattern.

This positive and productive use of thought experiments for explanatory purposes in contexts of what ultimately came to be known as "hypothetico-deductive" reasoning represents their oldest and no doubt most familiar employment.

3. ANAXIMANDER OF MILETUS

One of the most common uses of explanatory thought experiments proceeds by way of *analogy*. For example, in discussing why Thales' younger contemporary Anaximander of Miletus (b. ca. 610 B.C.), maintained that the earth is at the world's center, Aristotle attributes to him the following reasoning: "[T]hus if the earth now stays in place through the operation of a force, it too comes together at the center by being carried there because of the vortex" (*De Caelo*, B 13, 295a7; Kirk & Raven, p. 127). Here we clearly have the reasoning: "In vortices, objects tend to the center; let us suppose the world to be vortex-like; clearly this would explain that a large solid object like the earth would come to be positioned at the center." The thesis here supported by means of the analogy is clearly being argued for by the same method of explanatory thought-experimentation that we have been considering in the context of Thales.

However, in Anaximander we also find another, negatively demonstrative use of thought experimentation that is quite different from such explanatory employment. Thus consider the following justification for Anaximander's contention that "the earth stays aloft, held up by nothing, but remaining in place on account of its similar distance from all things" (Hippolytus, *Refutatio haeresium*, 1, 6, 3. Kirk & Raven, p. 134):

> It stays still because of its equilibrium. For it behooves that which is established at the center, and is equally related to the extremes, not to be borne one whit more either up or down or to the sides. (Aristotle, *De Caelo* B13, 295b10; Kirk & Raven p. 134.)

The reasoning thus takes the line that if the earth were not at the center, then it would eventually succumb to a tendency to move it further in one direction or another, and so would not have a stably fixed and firm position at all. This use of thought experimentation exhibits the following sort of structure:

METHOD NO. 2 (Negatively Demonstrative Reasoning)

• To be shown that *P* (where we do not yet know whether *P* or not-*P*).

• Assume—as "thought experiment"—that not-*P*.

• Deduce *Q* on the basis of this assumption, where *Q* is some patently false thesis.

• Hence maintain that *P*.

This negatively demonstrative employment of thought experiments may be characterized as their *refutatory* use. It is based on the well-known principle of indirect or "apagogical" reasoning that concludes negatively where a correlative positivity entails a false consequence. This reasoning is aptly characterized in Alexander Gottlieb Baumgarten's *Logica* as "*demonstratio falsitatis alicuius propositionis ex sequentibus ex illa falsis*" (sect. 691).

This sort of recourse to thought experimentation also recurs in the following remarks of Aristotle's regarding Anaximander:

Belief in the apeiron ("the unlimited") would result for those who consider the matter ... [inter alia] because only so would generation and destruction not fail, if there were an infinite source from which coming-to-be is derived. (Physics, Bk. Gamma, 4; 203b15; Kirk & Raven, p. 112.)

The derivation of a patently false conclusion (the termination by this time of all natural process) from an assumption of the initial premiss—that the source of natural process is something finite—is taken to establish the falsity of that premiss.

Again, Aristotle attributes to Anaximander the following reasoning for holding that the composition of the *apeiron* is something different from the four elements:

They [the four elements] are in opposition to one another—air is cold, water moist, [earth dry,] and fire hot—and therefore if any one of them were itself the infinite *apeiron*, the others would already have been destroyed. (*Physics*, Bk. Gamma, 5; 204b22; Kirk & Raven, p. 112.)

Clearly what we have here is once more the derivation of a patently false conclusion ("There is only one 'element' in nature; the rest have vanished long ago") from an assumption of the initial premiss—that one of the elements is itself to be identified with the inexhaustible *apeiron*. Here, exactly as in the preceding case, Aristotle attributes to Anaximander a line of reasoning which derives a patently false conclusion from the hypothetical assumption of the thesis whose falsity is to be established—a mode of persuing that clearly proceeds by way of a thought experiment.

Another example is present in the following passage:

Further he [Anaximander] says that in the beginning man was born from creatures of a different kind; because other creatures are soon self-supporting, but man alone needs prolonged nursing. For this reason he would not have survived if this [present one] had been his original form. (Pseudo-Plutarch, *Stromata*, 2; Kirk & Raven, p. 141.)

Here the negatively probative use of thought experimentation is once more at work. On the available evidence, this refutatory use of thought experiments was a favorite method of Anaximander's.

4. THE PYTHAGOREANS

In the school of Pythagoras of Samos (b. ca. 570 B.C.), the negatively probative mode of hypothetical reasoning came to be transmuted into a formal
mathematical method of proof—the mode of demonstration that has come
to be known as *reductio ad absurdum* argumentation. It is based on the
following line of reasoning:

METHOD NO. 3 (*Reductio ad Absurdum*)

- To be demonstrated that *P*.

- Assume—as "thought experiment"—that not-*P*.

- Deduce an outright contradiction from this assumption (this is generally
  effected by deducing *P* itself).

- Hence establish *P*.

The notorious proof of the incommensurability of the diagonal of a square
with its sides—the great Pythagorean secret for whose betrayal Hippasus
of Metapontium was, according to tradition, expelled from the Pythagorean
school (and perhaps even drowned at sea)—was accomplished by just this
device. It remains to this day the standard way of establishing the irrationality of the square root of two—one assumes the contrary as a working hypothesis and derives a contradiction. *Reductio* clearly represents a further
development in the use of thought experiments—the transmutation of the
negativity-productive mode of thought experimentation into a formal
method of mathematical proof.

5. XENOPHANES OF COLOPHON

Xenophanes of Colophon (b. ca. 570 B.C.) also resorted to the explanatory use of thought experiments:

> Xenophanes thinks that a mixing of the earth with the sea is going on, and that in time the earth is dissolved by the liquid. [Earlier there was a reverse phase of solidification of the sea.] He says that he has proofs of the following kind: shells are found inland, and in the mountains and in the quarries of Syracuse he says that an impression of a fish and of seaweed can be found, while an impression of a bayleaf was found in Pharos in the depth of the rock, and in Malta flat shapes of all marine objects. These, he says, were produced when everything was long ago covered with mud, and the impression was dried in the mud. (Hippolytus, *Ref.* I, 14, 5; Kirk & Raven, p. 177).

This passage clearly shows that Xenophanes sought to substantiate his doctrine of alternative phases of solidification and dissolution through the use of thought experiments by way of explanatory conjectures.

However, Xenophanes also introduced an important innovation. He inaugurated a style of *sceptical* use of thought experimentation. The salient thesis of Xenophanes affords the classical instance of this sort of reasoning:

> But if cattle and horses or lions had hands, or could draw with their hands and do the works that men can do, then horses would draw the forms of the gods like horses, and cattle like cattle, and they would make their bodies such as they each had themselves. (Kirk & Raven, p. 169, fragment 15; Clement, *Stromata*, v, 109, 3.)

This style of reasoning may be depicted as follows:

METHOD NO. 4 (Sceptical Thought Experimentation)

• Things being as they are, we incline to accept that *P* must be true.

• But suppose—by way of a "thought experiment"—that our situation were appropriately different (*as mutatis mutandis* it well might be).

• Then we would not accept *P* at all, but rather something else that is incompatible with *P*.

- Hence we aren't really warranted in our categorical acceptance of *P* (seeing that, after all, this is merely a contingent aspect of our particular, potentially variable situation).

What we have here is a resort to thought experimentation as an instrumentality of thought that is powerfully sceptical in its impetus.

Consider, for another example, the following argument presented by Xenophanes:

If god had not made yellow honey, men would consider figs far sweeter. (Kirk & Raven, p. 180, fragment 38.)

The reasoning of this last passage answers to the pattern:

1. Things being as they are, honey is "the sweetest thing in the world"—the very epitome of sweetness.

2. But suppose that honey didn't exist.

3. Then figs would be the sweetest thing we know of, so that *they* would be the epitome of sweetness.

4. Hence we should not maintain that honey is actually the epitome of sweetness; it merely happens to be the sweetest thing we happen to know of.

This argumentation also clearly instantiates the procedure of Method No. 4.

Xenophanes repeatedly employed this general technique to support his deeply sceptical position to the effect that:

No man knows, or ever will know, the truth about the gods and about everything I speak of: for even if one chanced to say the complete truth, yet one knows it not. Seeming is wrought over all things. (Frag. 34; Kirk & Raven p. 179.)

The very formulation of the position reflects the use of the thought experiment: "Suppose even that we asserted the full truth on some topic. The fact still remains that we would not be able to identify it as such." In this way, Xenophanes relied on thought experiments to establish the relativity of human knowledge, a device that was later to prove a major armament in the arsenal of the Sceptics.

6. HERACLITUS OF EPHESUS

Of all the Presocratics, however, it was Heraclitus of Ephesus (b. ca. 540) to whom thought experimentation came the most naturally. In his thought, the projection of "strange" suppositions is a prominent precept of method:

> If one does not expect the unexpected, one will not make discoveries [of the truth], for it resists discovery and is paradoxical. (Frag. 18/7; Burnet, p. 133; Kirk & Raven, p. 195.)[5]

Sometimes, Heraclitus' epigrams have the lucid pungency of proverbial wisdom:

> [Offered the choice,] donkeys would choose straw rather than gold. (Frag. 9/51; Burnet p. 137.)

A nice thought experiment this—who, after all, ever did, or would, offer gold to a donkey!? Here, then, we have a Xenophanes-reminiscent argument for a Xenophanes-reminiscent relativism.

Frequently, however, we find Heraclitus proceeding to earn his nickname of "the obscure." The following thought experiment is an example:

> If all things were turned to smoke, the nostrils would distinguish them. (Frag. 7/37; Burnet, p. 136).

It is not all that clear just what we are to make of this. But one construction is that we here again have a sceptical line of thought akin to the relativistic deliberations of Xenophanes: "Were all things smoky, the information we could obtain about them would be limited to what we can learn by smelling. Reality thus eludes the senses—and accordingly our knowledge as well. For our information about things is limited to their sensory aspect alone, and sense experience provides only information geared strictly and solely to the correlatively sensory aspect of things."

Heraclitus was also given to thought experimentation of the following essentially analogical format:

METHOD NO. 5 (Analogical Thought Experimentation)

- Suppose someone did X.

- Then (one would say that) he is F (mad, bad, or the like).

- But doing Y is just like doing X in the F-relevant regards.

- Therefore (one should also say that) someone who does Y is F.

Examples of this line of reasoning are as follows:

They vainly purify themselves by defiling themselves with blood, just as if one who had stepped into the mud were to wash with mud. Anyone who saw him doing this would deem him mad. (Frag. 5/129 & 130; Burnet, p. 145; Kirk & Raven, p. 211.)

For if it were not to Dionysius that they make the procession and sing the phallic hymn, the deed would be most shameless.... (Frag. 15/127; Burnet, p. 141; Kirk & Raven, p. 211.)

And they pray to these statues as though one were to talk to houses, not realizing the true nature of gods or demi-gods. (Frag. 5/126; Burnet, p. 141; Kirk & Raven, p. 211.) ((NR—recheck *horses?*))

All of these passages exemplify the analogical use of thought experimentation described in the preceding paradigm. (We could call someone who tries to clear away mud with mud crazy; what then of those who try to clear away blood with blood; will we not have to call them too crazy?) This analogy-exploiting, critical use of thought experimentation is clearly something quite different from its explanatory use as exemplified in Thales.

Thought experimentation of this sort is evidently a useful tool for a thinker who maintains the Heraclitean thesis that:

> To God all things are fair and good and right, though men hold some
> things wrong and some right. (Frag. 102/61; Burnet, p. 137.)

And so Heraclitus repeatedly uses thought experiments to expose what he
saw as deficiencies in contemporary religious practice, continuing the critique of early Greek religiosity launched by Xenophanes.

Heraclitus also employed thought experiments to argue that if reality
differed in a certain respect, things could not be as they are in other, correlative respects:

> If the sun did not exist, it would (always) be night (despite all the other
> stars). (Frag. 99/31; Burnet, p. 135.)

Or again:

> The learning of many things teaches not understanding, else would it
> have taught Hesiod and Pythagoras, and again Xenophanes and
> Hekataios. (Frag. 401/16; Burnet, p. 134.)

These thought experiments answer to the argumentative pattern of Method
2 above.

We learn from Aristotle's *Eudemian Ethics* (H1, 1235a25) that, according to Heraclitus:

> Homer [*Iliad*, XVIII, 107] was wrong in saying "Would that strife
> might perish from among gods and men" for there would be no musical
> scale unless high and low existed, nor living creatures without male and
> female, which are opposites [and all things would be destroyed]. (Frag.
> 22/43; Burnet, p. 136; Kirk & Raven, p. 196).

Here again we have a straightforward instance of Method 2, a refutatory
(negatively probative) use of hypothetical reasoning. This method too was
apparently a favorite of Heraclitus!

However, there is also a different style of characteristically Heraclitean
thought argumentation that is prominent in his thought:

METHOD NO. 6 (Value Dominance Argumentation)

- Assume—by way of a "thought experiment"—that *X* did not exist.

• Establish that in this event we could not even form the conception of *Y*, seeing that *X* and *Y* are correlative concepts (hot/cold, cause/effect, etc.).

• Conclude that therefore *Y*'s place in the overall scheme of things cannot be less important or valuable than *X*'s.

Heraclitus uses this sort of reasoning repeatedly to argue for the mutual dependence of opposites:

> Men would not have known the name of justice if these things [that people deem unjust] were not. (Frag. 23/60, Burnet, p. 137).

And again:

> It is not good for men to get all they wish to get. It is sickness that makes health pleasant; evil, good; hunger, satiety; weariness, rest. (Frag. 111/104; Burnet, p. 140.)

Presumably, in these cases the point is not that in the circumstances no *instances* of the opposite (sickness and importance) could not be found. The point is, rather, that there just is not work for the contrast-conception at issue to do in such a situation, a consideration that would render its introduction altogether pointless.

This style of argumentation is evidently tailor-made for a thinker who held that the mutual interdependence of opposites establishes the co-equal importance of the conceptions at issue:

> Men do not know how what is at variance agrees with itself. It is an attunement of opposite tensions, like that of the bow and the lyre. (Frag. 51/45; Burnet, p. 136.)

Here, thought experimentation along the indicated lines can be used to show that in removing the tension, we destroy also the very object that is at issue.

As these considerations show, Heraclitus was a devoted practitioner of thought experimentation, given to extracting far-reaching conclusions from fact-contravening hypotheses. The circumstance that we learn useful lessons about what is by projecting assumptions about what is not is clearly congenial to a thinker who maintains that "Nature loves to hide" (Frag. 123/10; Burnet, p. 133). Heraclitus was deeply persuaded that it is ultimately by mind (which can contemplate what is not) rather than by vision (which can only contemplate what is) that the deepest truths are to be learned. This "Heraclitean" view of the matter has much to be said for it, and anyone who shares it is bound to think highly of thought experimentation as a cognitive instrument of substantial value.

7. CODA

In concluding, it warrants reemphasis that thought experimentation is an important and flexible intellectual resource that has many varieties and allows very different sorts of employment. Our survey has shown the extent to which this cognitive resource was pioneeringly employed by the nature-philosophers of Presocratic Greece as a salient methodological device for developing their ideas. Though their interest was in reality, their deliberations about it placed extensive reliance on the use of problematic hypotheses in thought experimentation. Interestingly enough, "fiction" first made its way into Greek thought not in the setting of *belles lettres*, but in that of natural philosophy. For the Presocratics, conjecture was not a creative activity pursued for its own speculative interest, but an instrumentality for the investigation of the realm of truth and reality.

Someone might perhaps be tempted to think that the success which the Greek nature-philosophers had with *thought* experimentation exerted a dampening influence on their development of *real* experimentation. But this would be both unjust and inappropriate. For if the perspective attributed to Mach at the outset of this discussion is anything like correct, the development of thought experimentation is in fact an essential *preliminary* to the development of real experimentation as such.

The history of different styles of argumentation and reasoning has yet to be written. When it is, the Presocratics are clearly destined to obtain a good deal of credit. For the *methods of thought* they pioneered have been no less important and influential than then *substantive theories* they introduced.[6]

NOTES

[1] Sometimes thought experimentation is taken to call for a supposition that is known or believed to be false. But this is in fact only one, particularly strong form of thought experiment. When the detective reasons, "Now suppose that the butler did it ...," at some early stage of the investigation, his reasoning is clearly not unraveled as a thought experiment if it eventually turns out that he indeed did so.

[2] "Ueber Gedankenexperimente" in *Erkenntnis und Irrtum* (Leipzig, 1906), pp. 183-200 [see p. 187].

[3] For an interesting discussion of scientific thought experiments see T.S. Kuhn, "A Function for Thought Experiments in Science," in Ian Hacking (ed.), *Scientific Revolutions* (Oxford, 1981), pp. 6-27. More generally see Roy Sorensen, *Thought Experiments* (Oxford: Oxford University Press, 1992) as well as the present author's *What If? Thought Experiments in Philosophy* (New Brunswick, NJ: Transaction Books, 2005).

[4] In general, Presocratic texts are quoted in the translations given in G.S. Kirk and J.E. Raven, *The Presocratic Philosophers* (Cambridge, 1957). For the exception to this rule see footnote 5.

[5] The fragments of Heraclitus are here numbered in the order: Diels/Bywater. I have generally adopted Bywater's translation as improved by John Burnet, *Early Greek Philosophy* (London, 1892; 4th ed. 1930). But see also G.S. Kirk, *Heraclitus: The Cosmic Fragments* (Cambridge, 1954).

[6] This chapter is a revised version of an essay originally contributed to Gerald M. Massey and Tamara Horowitz (eds.), *Thought Experiments in Science and Philosophy* (Savage MD, 1991).

Chapter 4

GREEK SCEPTICISM'S DEBT TO THE SOPHISTS

1. INTRODUCTION

It is difficult to exaggerate the debt owed by the ancient Greek Sceptics to their Sophist precursors. For the fact is that most of the epistemological teachings that we nowadays deem characteristic of Greek scepticism were either originated by the Sophists, or were owed by Sophists and Sceptics alike to other ancient thinkers—such as Heraclitus of Ephesus—who formed part of their common heritage.[1] But while the Sophists anticipated much of what contemporary students of the subject find particularly engaging in the Sceptics, they also held some distinctive and interesting views of their own that the Sceptics lost sight of because they had other fish to fry. The Sophists accordingly deserve far more credit than has generally come their way.[2] (They never have and never shall recover from the misfortune of having their ideas come to be seen by posterity through the eyes of their most implacable opponent, Plato.[3])

2. THE PHENOMENA: THE TEN SCEPTICAL TROPES OF AENESIDEMUS

The *tropes* of ancient Greek scepticism were lines of thought designed to substantiate the doctrines of Pyrrho (ca. 360-275 B.C.), the somewhat shadowy founder of the sceptical school.[4] They were *apories,* that is, paradoxical considerations designed to manifest the infeasibility of obtaining secure knowledge about the world.[5] For such knowledge is supposed to be objective and impersonal—uniformly true and valid for all people—whereas the tropes indicate that such solidity is unrealizable in matters relating to this world of ours. It thus emerges that knowledge of reality is unattainable.

Sextus Empiricus presented us with a catalogue of ten of these tropes (*Pyrr. Hyp.* I 36 ff) presumably going back to Aenesidemus, who restored Pyrrhonism to prominence in the first century B.C. They stand as follows:

1 *affective variation*: idiosyncratic differences in the things giving people pleasure and pain, and in being beneficial or harmful to them.

2. *desire variation*: idiosyncratic differences in the needs and wants of people, in what they wish for or desire.

3. *sensory variation*: idiosyncratic differences in people's perceptual reaction to the same things and situations.

4. *state variation*: differences among individual people in their condition in matters of joy/sorrow, youth/maturity, love/hate, etc.

5. *societal variation*: differences among human groups in their customs, laws, beliefs, etc.

6. *contextual variability*: stones are lighter in water than in air, objects have different coloration at sunset than at mid-day, etc.

7. *optical variability*: in some environments, straight things appear bent, near things distant, etc.

8. *quantitative variability*: a small patch of a color may appear light, a larger one darker; a small quantity of wine enlivens, a larger one somnifies; a little food energizes a person, a lot dulls him, etc.

9. *familiarity variability*: in settings where events of a particular sort are common (earthquakes, floods), they are seen as normal and unsurprising, where they are rare they are seen as extraordinary and ominous.

10. *relational variability*: things are not light or heavy as such but lighter than some and heavier than others, and the same with strong/weak, great/small, high/low, etc. All things are what they are relative to the mind: *panta hôs pros tên dianoian.*

Even cursory inspection suffices to make it clear that these ten items fall into three groups:

A. Those turning on the fact that different individuals will systematically respond differently to the same things (no's 1-4),

B. Those indicating that different cultures will systematically respond differently to the same things (no. 5).

C. Those turning on the fact that one and the same individual will, in different circumstances and contexts, respond differently to the same things (no's. 6-10).

The three factors at issue may be characterized as personal variation, cultural relativity, and circumstantial variability, respectively.

It has to be acknowledged, however, that all three of these considerations antedate the sceptics. They were, in fact, part of the common currency of Sophistical teachings, as the following observations clearly indicate.

• *Personal variation*

While the import of personal variation found exponents as early as Heraclitus, it came to prominence with Protagoras' insistence on "to each his own." Thus in Plato's *Theaetetus* (152a), Socrates asks Theaetetus if he has read Protagoras' declaration that "Man is the measure of all things, of the things that are that they are, and of the things that are not that they are not." "Often," runs the reply. "Then," Socrates continues, "you know that he puts it something like this, that as something appears to me, so it *is* to me, and as it appears to you, so it *is* to you—you being a man and I too." (This addition is made in much the same words in the *Cratylus* at 386a— and compare *Euthydemus* 286e.) That this teaching was a key part of Protagoras's own argument is borne out by Aristotle:

> Protagoras said that man is the measure (*metron*) of all things, meaning simply and solely that what appears to each man assuredly also *is*. If this be so, it follows that the same thing both *is* and is *not*, and is both bad and good, and whatever else is asserted in contrary statements, since often a particular thing appears good or beautiful (*kalon*) to some and the opposite to others; and the measure is what appears to each individual. (*Metaph.* 1062b13.)

Plato glossed *measure* (*metron*) as *criterion* (*kriterion*, standard of judgment). (See *Theaetetus* 178b and cf. Sextus Empiricus, *Pyrr. Hyp.* 1.216.) And in the *Theaetetus* (152b), he explained the man-measure doctrine of Protagoras as meaning that the wind *is* cold to the person to whom it seems cold and warm to the person to whom it seems so.   As Sextus Empiricus tells us, Protagoras taught that:

> Men apprehend different things at different times owing to their differing dispositions; for he who is in a natural state apprehends those things subsisting in matter which are able to appear to those in a natural state, and those who are in a non-natural state. Moreover, precisely the same account applies to the variations due to age, and to the sleeping or waking state, and to each several kind of condition. Thus according to him, man becomes the criterion of things that are; for all things that appear to men also are, and things that appear to no man, also are without being. (*Pyrr. Hyp.* I, 218.)

Person-to-person variation in apprehending the properties of things evidently lay at the heart of Protagoras' position; our sources agree that, on Protagoras' view, what appears to each individual is, for him, the only "reality." And in general, the Greek Sophists saw the idiosyncratic cognitive posture of each particular individual as a force to be reckoned with.

• *Cultural relativity*

Cultural relativism was yet another mainstay of Greek intellectual tradition.   Not only do we find it in such writers as Herodotus, but, as our sources amply indicate, statements expressing views along these lines were standard among the Greek Sophists, who taught that in matters of inquiry we can never achieve secure knowledge (*epistêmê*) but only opinion (*doxa*) reflecting the views of people. For example, in sect. 13 of his *Encomium of Helen* (ca. 370 B.C.) Gorgias stressed three forms of cognitive relativism: (1) the different schools of "physicists" each espousing its own idiosyncratic view of the universe, (2) the different "tendencies of opinion" of different groups in public matters, each exhibiting its own likes and prejudices on matters of public debates on the law and on the Assembly, and (3) the different schools of philosophical opinion, each with its own characteristic theories and doctrines. Evaluative issues in particular are always a matter of one's point of view: for the Greeks the fall of Troy was a triumph, for the Trojans a tragedy, as the Sophistic tract *Dissoi Logoi* has it (DK 90).[6] As Protagoras says, to the sick man food is sour, to the healthy man sweet (*Theaetetus* 166e).

• *Circumstantial variability*

The Protagoras of Plato's dialogue of that name waxes eloquent on the issue of the variability of things with respect to circumstance and context:

Some [things beneficial to men] have no effect on animals, but only on trees. Again, some are good for the roots of trees but injurious to the young growths. Manure, for instance, is good for all plants when applied to their roots, but utterly destructive if put on the shoots or young branches. Or take olive oil. It is very bad for plants, and most inimical to the hair of all animals except man, whereas men find it of service both to their hair and to the rest of the body. So diverse and multiform is goodness that even with us the same thing is good when applied externally but deadly when taken internally. All doctors forbid the sick to use oil in preparing their food, except in the smallest quantities. (Plato, *Protagoras*, 333e-334e.)

The evidence amply indicates that the differential response of an individual to one and the same thing in different circumstantial contexts was also a commonplace of Sophistical teaching. The *Dissoi Logoi*, for example, insists that people deem nothing good or bad exceptionlessly, but the matter depends on the context and the "point of view." (DK 90).

In sum, then, the tropes of Aenesidimus—those salient phenomena on which the sceptics based their view of the unaccessibility of the physical world to human knowledge—were a staple of the intellectual diet of the Sophistical predecessors of scepticism.

3. THE MAIN CONCLUSIONS DRAWN FROM THE PHENOMENA

From the phenomena suggestive of our incapacity to determine through our sensory experiences a fixed nature of things independently of person, society, and context, the Greek Sceptics of the Pyrrhonian school drew three major conclusions regarding our prospects of obtaining knowledge of the world:

1. *Isostheneia*: the equivalence status of alternative positions. Different individuals and groups have their own view of the world's things, each of which is just as appropriate and justified as any other. Throughout the domain of putative truth and reality, reason is impotent to establish any one conclusive result rather than another.

2. *Akatalêpsia*: the infeasibility of attaining knowledge/*epistêmê*, subject to the idea that "nothing can be known."[7]   The equivalidity of conflicting claims compels the abandonment of claims to knowledge. Nothing carries decisive conviction (*katalêpsis*).

3. *Epochê*: suspension of judgment and belief. The sensible thinker's reaction to the equivalency of alternative positions and the unattainability of reliable knowledge about things must be to suspend any and all judgment.[8]   The appropriate reaction when confronted with the alternative claims about reality is to refuse to commit oneself to any one of them—to abstain from belief. Human reason is too weak an instrument to provide knowledge. We must be prepared to live beliefless (*adoxastôs*, agnostically), accepting the sceptical line that the true nature of the world's affairs is simply unknowable.

Now as regards these doctrinal mainstays of Greek scepticism, it has to be acknowledged that such sceptical teachings were for the most part already integral components of Greek sophistry.

1. Isostheneia: Equivalency

The equivalency of different views is inherent in Protagoras' famous *homo mensura* doctrine that "man is the measure of all things, of that which is that it is, and of that which is not, that it is not." And it was on just this basis that Protagoras maintained his famous thesis that" on every topic there are two arguments, contrary to one another"—each assertion (*phasis*) has its equally tenable counterassertion (*apophasis*). The idea that claims to knowledge cannot be made good is also prominent in Gorgias teaching that even if something is, it cannot be comprehended by man since thought as such can never assure existence or reality. Gorgias' notorious thesis "that nothing is" was not so much a version of nihilism as an attempt to show that by the sort of reasoning one finds, for example, in the theories of Parmenides it is as easy to argue for "it is not" as for "it is."[9]   Thus Isocrates attacks paradox-mongers and eristics of all kinds, and goes on to say that everyone knows that Protagoras, Gorgias, Zeno, and Melissus have espoused views of this kind:

> Who could outdo Gorgias, who had the audacity to say that nothing is, or Zeno who tried to show that the same things were possible and impossible, or Melissus who amid the infinite profusion of things tried to find proofs that all is one? What they did demonstrate was that it is easy to trump up a false argument about whatever you like to put forward. (*Helen* 1; quoted from Guthrie, p. 195.)

Again, the *Phaedrus* (261d ff, cf. *Rep.* 453e) attributes to the Sophists a mode of reasoning he calls "antilogic" (*antilogikê*), which consists in opposing one *logos* to a contrary *logos*, invoking such opposed arguments to maintain opposite conclusions regarding things or states/affairs (as being, say, both just and unjust or both honest and dishonest). (Compare also Socrates condemnation of the "misologists" in the *Phaedo*, 89d ff.) Then too, the unattributable sophistic tract on "Twofold Arguments" (*Dissoi Logoi*, DK 90) begins with the contention that "Twofold arguments concerning the good and the bad are put forward in Greece by those who pursue philosophy," and the following paragraphs begin similarly but instance, respectively, the beautiful and the ugly, the just and the unjust, and the true and the false, in each case presenting opposing judgments of seemingly equal merit.

With reference to the laws and customs of nations, barbarians as well as Greeks, the Sophist Hippias taught that these are simply the product of affinity and familiarity, and that it is not appropriate to regard one as of itself any better than any other. We should refrain from any judgment of inherent superiority. Similarly, Diogenes Laertius tells us that the *antilogic* of Protagoras projected the theory that there are dissonant *logoi* or accounts to be given of everything, and that a good reasoner is always able "to make the lesser (or weaker) argument the stronger," so that it is possible to refute or undermine any claim to factuality by arguments no less good than those that support it (Diogenes Laertius, IX, 50 ff.).

2. *Akatalêpsia: Infeasibility of Knowledge*

The infeasibility of authentic knowledge about the world is of course a major Leitmotiv of Greek sophistical teaching. Thus Gorgias' treatise which, according to Sextus Empiricus, was entitled "On That Which is Not or On Nature," has as one of its central theses that nothing can be comprehended by men. (Sextus Empiricus, *Adv. Log.* 1.65-87.) Gorgias' argument seems to have run as follows: "Whatever is thought is merely thought, and will not, as such, be actually real. Hence reality cannot be thought—the only thing that can be thought, being thought. And therefore really cannot be known, seeing that knowing consists in thinking something to be such-and-such." (See Sextus Empiricus, *Adv. Log.* 1.77 ff.[10]) The point is that thought is only able to grasp thoughts and not extramental reality: thought and language cannot present a reality external to themselves. We are never entitled to say that something in actuality "is *F*" or "is not *F*" in nature.[11] Sextus Empiricus depicted Gorgias together with Protagoras as having destroyed the *kriterion* or standard of judgment (*Adv. Math.* 7.65), with the result that no means was left of establishing what was true. And the pseudo-Aristotelian treatise "On Mellisus, Xenophanes, and Gorgias" also insists that Gorgias sought to abolish "the criterion" of knowledge, denying that we possess any effective standard (*kriterion*) for genuine *epistêmê* (MXG 980a9ff).[12] Again, in the *Theaetetus* (172b) Socrates informs us that Protagoras taught that as regards the honorable or dishonorable, just or unjust, and pious or impious, no state is wiser (*sophôteron*) than another seeing that such things do not have an intrinsic nature (*phusis*) of their own but only obtain such features relative to common opinion (consensus, *to koinêi doxa*).[13] Likewise, in the *Phaedrus* (267a), Socrates is chagrined that Gorgias and his fellow rhetoricians "held the plausible (*ta eikota*, the likely-seeming) in more honor than the true." Thus for the Sophists, exactly as for the Sceptics, the human cognitive situation is seen as leaving us no alternative but to settle for something less than the real truth of things. One does not have to go far in the study of Greek Sophistry—indeed not beyond Gorgias himself—to see that the sophists were every bit as sceptical about the claims of human knowledge to depict reality as were the sceptics.

3. *Epochê*

At this point, however, the Sophists took a line that differed markedly from that of the Sceptics. For while the sceptics advocated *epochê*—the suspension of judgment and belieflessness—the Sophists opted for social conformity and consensus, for acquiescing in the dominant view of our society. And so the scepticism of the Sophists did not issue in belieflessness (in suspensive *epochê* and cognitive vacuity) but in social acceptance. The scepticism of the Greek Sceptics took the nihilistic line "Authentic knowledge is unachievable; therefore, since any opinion is as defective as any other, we should affirm nothing." By contrast, the scepticism of the Greek Sophists took a relativistic line: "Authentic knowledge is unachievable, therefore, since any opinion is as good as any other, we should acquiesce in the dominant view of the group." The Sophists, in sum, were prepared to let public consensus stand surrogate for knowledge.

* * *

The overall import of these considerations is clear, however. Just as the *data* for scepticism with respect to knowledge about the world (i.e. the sceptical *tropes*) were already prominent in teachings of the Sophists, so also were most of the principal *doctrines* that constitute the core of negativism with respect to knowledge of nature. For the Sophists, as for the Sceptics, the world as we can experience it is a manifold of appearances that leaves any prospect of authentic knowledge of reality beyond our reach. Both positions are sceptical—but with a significant difference. The scepticism of the Greek Sceptics was nihilistic; it was oriented to *epochê*—to a total abstinence from judgment. But the scepticism of the Greek Sophists was limited: it was negative on the cognitive side as regards actual knowledge of the true nature of things, but positive on the conventional side as regards the acceptability of matters of human agreement. It allowed the social consensus of the *vox populi* to substitute for what rational inquiry could not provide. And, of course, the prospect (and reality) of diverse compacts in different groups prevailed in the direction of relativism. And so while Greek Scepticism was nihilistic, Greek Sophistry was relativistic.

4. EXPANSIONS: THE PERVASIVENESS OF THE SOPHISTS' SCEPTICISM

To be sure, there was much more to Greek Scepticism than a negative view of the prospects of knowledge regarding the natural world around us. For the Sceptics also extended their negation of knowledge from the sphere of nature into other regions: religion, philosophy, mathematics, etc. But in this rejection of theorizing in general the Sceptics were once again anticipated by the Sophists.

(1) *Social affairs.* The idea that each nation has its own laws, customs, and social norms—its own modus operandi as regards the just, right, and proper—found a vivid expression already in Herodotus, the "father of history," who characterized the phenomenon at issue in vivid terms:

> [I]f one were to offer men to choose out of all the customs in the world such as seemed to them the best, they would examine the whole number, and end by preferring their own; so convinced are they that their own usages far surpass those of all others . . . . Unless, therefore, a man was mad, it is not likely that he would make sport of such matters . . . . That people have this feeling about their laws may be seen by very many proofs, among others, by the following: Darius, after he had got the kingdom, called into his presence certain Greeks who were at hand, and asked—"What he should pay them to eat the bodies of their fathers when they died?" To which they answered, that there was no sum that would tempt them to do such a thing. He then sent for certain Indians, of the race called Callatians, men who eat their fathers, and asked them, while the Greeks stood by, and knew by the help of an interpreter all that was said—"What he should give them to burn the bodies of their fathers at their decease?" The Indians exclaimed aloud, and bade him forbear such language. Such is men's wont herein; and Pindar was right, in my judgment, when he said, "Custom is the king o'er all." (*The History of Herodotus*, tr. by George Rawlinson [New York, 1859-61], Bk. III, ch. 38.)

And Plato ascribed to the protagonist of his *Protagoras* (325e ff), the view that justice and norms are no more than a particular society's means to social control. Along just these lines, the Sophist *Cratylus* taught that all of the laws of different states are equally good (Plato, *Cratylus* 429b).

(2) *Ethics and aesthetics.* Plato indicates that for Protagoras the doctrine that "man is the measure" applies also for such moral and aesthetic characterizations as "right" and "beautiful," so that (for example) "whatever seems just to a city is right for that city so long as it seems so" (*Theaetetus* 172 a). Again, a straightforward version of ethical relativism was attributed to Prodicus in the pseudo-Platonic dialogue the *Eryxias*. He is described as arguing that what is good for one man is not good for another man, so that we cannot speak of anything as good *simpliciter*. A thing will be good in relation to one person and not good in relation to an-

other, according to the person and the way that person is connected with the thing at issue.

(3) *Religion.* Protagoras wrote a treatise *On the Gods* whose opening lines ran:

I have no capacity knowing about the gods, whether they are or are not, nor what they are like in form. There are many impediments to knowledge of the matter, including the obscurity of the subject matter and the brevity of life. (Diogenes Laertius, IX, 51; cf. Eusebius, *Praeparatio Evangelica* 14.3.7)

Prodicus attributed the origin of men's belief in gods to psychological and naturalistic causes—especially a deification of the useful (Sextus Empiricus, *Adv. Phys* 1.18), while Critias maintained that gods were invented deliberately by men to render their unruly fellows tractable by putting the "fear of God" into them.

(4) *Philosophy.* The Sophists were opposed to the whole project of philosophy as it had been practiced by their predecessors. Thus Gorgias seized on the mutual inconsistencies among the diverse accounts of the philosopher to betoken the untrustworthiness of the whole enterprise (See *Helen* 13). And Protagoras' critics took him to maintain that whatever seems true to a person is so for that person not only with respect to matters of sensation and evaluation but also with respect to philosophy. Just this was the point d'appui for the Socratic counter-critique later known as the *peritropê* or turning-of-the-tables, which argued that Progatoras, in maintaining that everybody's opinion is true for them, must thereby also acknowledge the truth of his opponents' belief that his own position is wrong (*Theaetetus* 171a-b, and note also the attribution of this argument to Democritus in DK 68A114).

(5) *Mathematics.* Protagoras called mathematical knowledge into serious question in an attack on the geometricians (DK 80B7). In particular he maintained that diagrams did not correspond to mathematical reality: when, for example, the geometer talks of a tangent touching a circle at just one point, he is not talking about realities because, in any concrete case, contact will always be made along a (diminutive) line segment (Aristotle, *Metaph.* 998a4).

As such considerations indicate, not only was scepticism about the world a position amply represented in the Sophistic school, but its expansion across the far wider domain of theories in general that were envisioned by Greek Scepticism was also amply prefigured by the Sophists. Like the Sceptics after them, the Sophists united the entire manifold of individual judgments, perspectives, points of view, outlooks, opinions, attitudes, and evaluations under the comprehensive rubric of "appearances" (*phainomena*). Thus Sextus Empiricus flatly credits Protagoras with the Sceptic's teaching that nothing exists for us humans but phenomena (*kai dia touto tithêsi ta phainomena hekostôi mona, kai houtôs eisagei to pros ti. dio kai dokei koinônian echein pros tous Pyrrôneious*; *Pyrr. Hyp.* I, 216 and cf. I, 219). And Aristotle also affirms that for Protagoras *metron d' einai to phainmenon hekastôi* (*Metaph.* 1062b19).

5. GREEK SOPHISTICAL DOCTRINE

There is good reason to think that the Sophists have suffered an undeservedly bad press among historians of philosophy and continue to be under appreciated by contemporary students of the history of Greek philosophy.[1] For, as a fair-minded examination of the data indicates, the Sophists had a coherent overall position based on more or less the following doctrinal views:

1. Actual knowledge of reality is unachievable.

2. What we humans need and want is guidance for living and acting in this world—for everyday *praxis*, in particular in contexts of social interaction.

3. Knowledge being unavailable, we can only get such guidance from a knowledge-external source.

4. And this non-cognitive guidance is in found in our *interest* (*sumpheron* = advantage, or *pleonexia* = self-advantage)—in our recognition of personal needs and wants.[15]   Practical efficacy being the key, this is something that should be judged by people in terms of their own advantage.

5. As regards the interests of individual people, "man is the measure" and everyone is their own arbiter, while at the societal level interest is determined for the group by its leadership or ruling establishment[16]— by the elite or "the stronger," as Thrasymachus has it in insisting that

the just is what lies "in the interest of the stronger" (*to tou kreittonos sumpheron, Republic* 341a). And Protagoras taught that people are the ultimate arbiters of their own interest—the definitive determiners of what is beneficial to them—even as what is lawful and proper in a state is whatever its own established customs and norms decree.[17] (It was, of course, against exactly this view that the Socratic distinction between people's real and their merely apparent interests was to be deployed.)

6. The proper and effective instrument for the leadership of a success-fully functioning state to use in imposing their view on the group as a whole is not force but persuasion. (The former process would yield a tyranny that is the very opposite of effective government.) To crux of effective governance is to have individuals *internalize* the group inter-est—to make the best interests of the community—the state, if you will—an integral part of their own best interests. And therefore rheto-ric is the key instrument of governance, discourse being the effective and proper instrument of persuasion.

A coherent overall stance was thus at issue in the position of the Sophists. And this stance comprised two components, a theoretical one (parts 1-3) and a practical one (parts 4-6). Now in its initial theoretical phase, the posi-tion of the Sophists actually included all of the central doctrines characteris-tic of Greek scepticism. Thus as concerns those particular doctrines that we would nowadays call "epistemological," Greek Sophistry and Greek Scepti-cism occupied much the same ground. And the elaborate discussion of the unavailability of a valid "criterion" of knowledge in Book I of Sextus Em-piricus' *Against the Logicians* makes it quite clear that the Sceptics them-selves were keenly aware and unblushingly accepting of their debt to such leading Sophists as Gorgias and Protagoras.[18]

Only when the question of the appropriate *response* to this agreed situa-tion in regard to its bearing upon matters of practice and action comes to the fore do the two schools reach a significant parting of the ways. For the Sceptics' principle was "to live by 'probability' (*pithanotês*, persuasive-ness)"—to proceed in life under the guidance of four "life-guards" (*hê biô-tikê têrêsis*): the direction of nature, the constraint of the passions, the heri-tage of usages and customs, and the instructions of the practical arts. (See Sextus Empiricus, *Pyrr. Hyp.* I 23-24.) The Sceptics thus plumped for yield-ing to the pressure of "irrational," unthinking forces: our inner personal

drives and the social pressure of established ways. The Sophists, by con
trast, insisted upon the centrality of interest. They did not propose to short
circuit reasoning and language-manipulating thought (*logos*), but geared it
operation to a pre- or sub-rational awareness of self-interest. Their guide t
life was reason operating under the direction of our witting appreciation o
our own best interests.

To see the difference more clearly, let us review the overall lay of th
land.

6. THEORY AND PRACTICE IN SCEPTICISM AND SOPHISTRY

The central theses of the present deliberations are two. The first is that *th*
theoretical anti-cognitivist component of Greek scepticism is something tha
was taken over lock, stock, and barrel from the Sophists. For as the preced
ing deliberations indicate, all of the principal teachings of the Sceptics re
garding the infeasibility of knowledge were already found in the teaching
of the Sophists.

Our second principal thesis is that, as best one can tell, the salient point a
which the Sceptics parted ways from the Sophists is the issue of scepticism'
operative consequences for human *praxis*. For what the Sceptics urged wa
a mental disengagement *(ataraxia), an epochê-geared detachment from*
judgmental thought in favor of living by "appearances." By contrast, wha
the Sophists proposed was: *a commitment through interests and the requi*
sites of effective of praxis as mediated through our personal sense of desir
ability and value. Instead of detachment, the Sophists urged taking a stanc
on the basis of how we individually size things up and approve them i
terms of what is suitable for us.

The practical component of radical Greek Scepticism pivoted on the con
sequences of the cognitive situation for our human *modus operandi* in thi
life. Its principal components were:

—mental detachment (*ataraxia*), agnosticism of mind and avoidance o
   cognitive commitment of any sort: being *adoxastôs* and dispensing
   with belief

—living by "appearances" (such appearances consisting in natural incli
   nations to think and the impulsion of bodily drives) and by the accus
   tomed ways of proceeding (the traditionary rules of the community—

its laws and customs), and the established *modus operandi* of practical endeavor such as the medical or the agricultural arts).[19]

The Pyrrhonian Sceptics thus looked to the governing impetus of "external" forces (nature's necessitation and social pressure). In effect, they said: "Don't commit yourself in matters of distant theory, but with issues of concrete thought and action just 'go with the flow' and yield to the pressure of your individual inclination and the established practices of your group."

By contrast, the Sophists said: "Do commit your beliefs but do so on your own terms—on the basis of your assessment based on personal value scheme rooted in your judgment of your own interests." They thus took a very different line. They placed prime stress upon our *interests*—our needs and wants, our internally conditional sense of our own good—to provide for what circumscribed nature would not of itself supply. Their view was that since there are no cogent externally imposed standards, we humans must get together to establish our own as best as we can manage through a rational assessment of our own interests. For the Sophists viewed each person as the final and ultimately decisive court of appeal where one's own interests are concerned. And thus they saw the social function of individual opinion as the key, and supported a life of praxis based on the guidance of a reflective view of our own personal *interests* as formed in the forum of public discussion.

Thus, while the Sceptics opted for individualistic mind-control and *ataraxia*, the Sophists proposed a shift into the social and political arena. As they saw it, the critical function of rhetoric is to provide the means by which a ruling elite can (and in a stable and healthy community must) make use of public discussion to induce its various members to internalize the interest of the larger whole as part of their own personal interest. Both schools alike were committed to conflict avoidance. But the Pyrrhonian sought to achieve it by refraining from committed and indulging in a quarrel-averting mental anaesthetics. The Sophists, on the other hand, thought to achieve such same end through group solidarity and acquiescence in the dominant opinions of the community as shaped under the pressure of a shared appreciation of interests.

The Sophists were as sceptical as any Sceptic about our ability to obtain secure knowledge regarding "the real world." And the problem they now faced in common was: Where do we go from there? The Sceptics opted for detachment—for *ataraxia*. Their counsel was that of cognitive despair—of a retreat into a pessimistic noncommitment as regards opinion formation.

The Sophists, by contrast, were optimistic. They had faith in the capacity of civilized society to create—through convention and consensus—a comfortable human home in a difficult and ultimately unintelligible world. For many or most practical purposes, so they thought, convention could be used as a surrogate for knowledge.

7. THE PROMISE OF RHETORIC: *NOMOS* VS. *PHUSIS*

Just like the Sceptics later on, the Sophists saw the project of Presocratic physical science about nature as having self-destructed in a proliferation of ultimately unvalidatable conflicting doctrines.[20]   But in reaction, they proposed a shift to the political sphere of people and their works, a sphere where rhetoric offers the means to a thought-coordination unavailable in the natural philosophy. Precisely because the exigencies of scepticism indicate that human minds cannot be coordinated with *reality*, it is crucial that they become coordinated *with one another* in the public forum. Accordingly, the use of language and rhetoric acquired paramount importance for Sophistical doctrine, since the value and importance of discussion was seen to lie in just this capacity to enlist voluntary conviction.

The Sophists combined their elitism with a democratic approach. They favored rule by a select few, but insisted that in a viable state those ruling few have to carry the many along—and willingly at that—through *convincing* them of the state's needs. Brute force will not serve the purpose. For force *compels* people while rhetoric *persuades* them; the one *constrains* them to subordinate their interests to those of others while the other *convinces* people to see where their interests lie. Compulsion rests on another's brute force, persuasion on another's capacity, and—as Protagoras puts it in Plato's dialogue, "I hold that capacity (*dunamis*) and brute force (*ischus*) are not the same, for capacity comes from knowledge (*epistêmê*) and inspiration (*mania*) and sensibility (*thumos*), but brute force comes from one's constitution—one's bodily physique" (350e ff). The Sophists were impressed by the capacity of custom (*nomos*) to supply —thanks to the persuasive power of language[21] —what nature (*phusis*) could not furnish: the common focussing of different minds in the consensus essential to a viable society.

The Sophists, in sum, looked to the creation of a public order through the voluntarily enlisted consensus of the populace emerging from an inner conviction engineered in the public interest by a sagacious elite through effective rhetoric. In their own way, the Sophists were the classical exponents of the polity of "the consent of the governed." But, as they saw it, this consent would have to be obtained through the persuasive use of language by people recognized as knowledgeable—and can *only* be obtained in this way. For Sophism, the crux is a consensus to which all citizens have a contribution to make—a social conformity of thought that offsets nature's variability. The Sophists were concerned for a "logic of assent" at work in the political process of public discourse to produce a uniformity or consensus neither constrained by nature nor enforced by logical demonstration, but engendered through discussion. Their teaching envisioned a language-rooted guile or trick (*apatê*)—a sleight of mind that substitutes a man-made uniformity for an unavailable objective uniformity that nature does not make available to us.[22] And so, with Prodicus, they saw themselves as operating (Plato's derision notwithstanding) "at the boundary of politics and philosophy" (*Euthydemus*, 305c). (The "social contract" theory of human society and politics begins its long and influential career in the social coordination theory of the Sophists.)

To us, Protagoras' thesis that the rhetorician can "make out the weaker argument to be the stronger" (Aristotle, *Rhetorica* 1402a23; Diogenes Laertius 9.51) or Gorgias' dictum that "persuasion with the aid of words can mold men's minds as it wishes" (*Helen* 13) have an ineradicably cynical tone. But for the Sophists this circumstance represented a saving road to political legitimacy, because of the value they placed concurrently on the persuasive cogency of the insight of the elite and the voluntary acceptance of the many. That the Sophistic art is an instrumentality for achieving the health of the body politic, since "as the physician produces change by means of medications, so the sophist does it by words" (*ho men iatros pharmakois metaballei, ho de sophistês logois*) is the teaching that Plato's Socrates puts in the mouth of Protagoras (*Theaetetus*, 167a).[23]

Of course, even as the physician cannot turn water into wine or poison into nourishment, so there are limits to what the rhetorician can be expected to accomplish with words. The clever orator may be able to lead people by the nose with regard to various issues but presumably not in matters that affect their own personal advantage. They are bound to have a fairly well-developed sense of self-advantage. The most that the accomplished rhetorician can expect to achieve is to induce people to accept the communal good, as he himself sees it, as forming part of their own interests.[24]

The very power and force of rhetoric means that in public discussion we have to put our faith in the power of argumentation to impact upon the common sense which all people share alike (*Protagoras*, 319d). As Protagoras puts it in Plato's dialogue: "When people meet for political consulta-

tion—where they should be guided throughout by justice and good sense—
they naturally allow everybody to contribute, since it is held that everyone
partakes of this virtue, or states would not exist" (323a). For Protagoras
everyone's opinion counts in these political matters and the "expert"—
though necessary—is no better than his capacity to convince his fellows
(and hence is useless without rhetorical skills). And to maintain trust, the
leaders must deserve it, for "life is not liveable for the man who has lost the
confidence of others; the man who loses his money or falls from power or
who is exiled from his country might get on his feet again, but he who
throws away good faith cannot regain it" (*Gorgias*, DK 11a, 21; Sprague, p
59). The political philosophy of the Sophists does not fall into the neat divi-
sions of Plato's taxonomy. It is neither an elitist/oligarchical rule of the favored few, nor a democratic rule of the many, but invokes a coordination or
combination of these positions by envisioning a situation in which the few
manage to rule only by *convincing* the many and maintaining their trust.

The prioritizing on rationality, reason, and reasoning is among the
greatest of ancient Greece's many gifts to European civilization. Rational
deliberation as the proper instrument of control over self, others, and nature was a key theme of classical Greek thought. In mathematics, in philosophy, and in public life the idea of rational conviction, argumentation
from evidence, and deciding from reasons was a hallmark of Greek thinking. Following in the tracks of the geometricians, the Sophists were the
first to put this commitment on the agenda in the public sector—that is
with regard to the conduct of public affairs. Reasoned argumentation and
persuasion, so the Sophists argued, is the proper instrumentability of human control: in mathematics, proof; in philosophy, demonstration; in politics, argument. This positive reliance on the power of reason put the Sophists at the pole opposite from the eventual negativism of the Sceptics. Reasoned argumentation is the best we can do, said the sceptics—and its not
good enough. The Sophists by contrast accentuated the positive: It is the
best we can do, they apparently held, and for that very reason has to be accepted as good enough.

8. LANGUAGE AND ITS PROBLEMS

To be sure, the Sophists were altogether sceptical about the capacity of language to depict reality—to facilitate a cognitive grasp of *phusis*. Thus Gorgias even insisted that hearer and speaker never have the same objective
thing in mind, since the same thing cannot, without losing its identity, be

present in more people than one—and even if it could, would not appear the same to both, since they are different from one another and in different places (MXG, 980b9ff). The logical terminus of this line of thought was the radical linguistic scepticism of Cratylus, a younger contemporary of Socrates (Plato, *Cratylus* 429d and 440a), whom Aristotle ridicules as holding that he ought to say nothing at all, but only move his finger, and as saying that Heraclitus did not go far enough in saying one cannot step twice into the same river because one could not do so even once (*Metaph.* 1010a10).[25] Cratylus seems to have taught (as one would expect from what is attributed to him in Plato's dialogue that to utter any statement is to commit oneself to the fatally flawed affirmation that something *is*. But this nihilistic extreme is definitely not the terminus to which orthodox Sophistry tended. And even Cratylus accepted that customary usage is the definitive arbiter of the meaning of words (Plato, *Cratylus* 430d and 436e).

The mainstream Sophists denied the serviceability of language only for real-world representation (of *phusis*) but certainly not for mind-to-mind communication (*via nomos*). They taught that while we cannot communicate about a *reality* that lies outside our mind's grasp, what we can communicate about "with our neighbors" is the manifold of what is encapsulated in language—the *logos* over which we are ourselves the masters within the ambit of our custom-forged community.[26] Communal consensus is our only standard of reality for, as Gorgias put it, "existence is not manifest if it does not involve opinion (*to dokein*), and opinion is unreliable if it does not involve existence."[27] For the Sophists, man is preeminently the social animal able to exist in a civilized society because *nomos* saves the day where *phusis* lets us down.[28] As Hippias puts it in Plato's *Protagoras*, a viable state must harmonize not only kinsmen and kindred spirits, who are linked by nature (*phusis*), but also dissimilars who have to be linked by law (*nomos*)—that "tyrant of men" (*turannos tôn anthrôpôn*)" (377c ff). For, as Lycophron taught, the law constitutes through convention a community in which it serves as "a guarantor of mutual rights" (Aristotle, *Politics* III, 5; 1280b8). Civilized society is a human artifact: in human affairs it is not the gods that provide for justice, "the greatest of goods among men," but we ourselves have to make shift to do the imperfect best we can in this regard.[29]

The inherent meaninglessness of sounds does not preclude agreement on their meaning as *words*, even as the smallness of the word does not prevent "large" from *meaning* just that. Such matters are not settled by the inherent nature of things—of which, in any case, we have no knowledge—they are matters of *nomos*, of convention. As Plato's Socrates informs us

(*Theaetetus* 172b), some Sophists held that *nomos* can, (though public con
sensus (to *koinêi doxa*), effectively determine what is true—at any rate for as
long as that consensus stands.

The linguistic scepticism of the Sophists thus has to be understood in the
light of their distinction between what is by *custom* (*nomos*) and what is by
nature (*phusis*). To be sure, they taught that human reason and language
(*logos*) cannot grasp reality—that it is impotent to capture the real truth of
things. But language is itself a creation of custom, designed not to put the
minds of men in touch with physical reality but to put them into touch with
one another. And while *reality* as such is something extra-human that lies
beyond the reach of our inadequate cognitive grasp, human conventions are
thought-things that we ourselves make and hence can understand and come
to terms with. Within this custom-established domain, language and *logos*
can function effectively as a means of interpersonal communication and so
cial coordination.

After a long lifetime of trying in vain to make sense of himself, his fel
lows, and his world, the American polymath Henry Adams concluded that
the world's realities are ultimately inaccessible to us seeing that "chaos was
the law of nature, order was the dream of man."[30]   This line of reflection
captures the scepticism of the ancient Sophists. For them, the world is a
chaos within which individual people and human societies struggle—with
mixed success at best—to create islands of intelligible order for themselves.
And where such intelligible order exists it is emphatically not a product of
natural process but of human contrivance.

As the Sophists saw it, the great service of rhetoric is as an instrument for
forming the consensus that is requisite to a viable social order. Thus according to Diogenes Laertius, Protagoras abandoned the idea of an understanding
(*dianoia*) that grasps the actual nature of the things referred to in discourse
in favor of reliance on the word or name (*onoma*) whose sense is generated
through the conventions that we ourselves introduce (Diogenes Laertius
9.52). People would—all of us—live as isolated prisoners in our own pri
vate world of personal experience and personal opinion if we did not make
use of persuasive language to break out of this isolation by coming to
agreement, by coordination and compact, by employing *custom* (*nomos*) to
provide by convention for a lawful uniformity that nature (*phusis*) itself does
not supply.

Interestingly enough, however, the Sophists—or at any rate Protagoras—
played a rather complex game with the *nomos/phusis* distinction in conse
quence of which it is not all that easy to locate their teaching along the tradi

tional realism/conventionalism axis. For while they saw norms as unqualifiedly conventional, they held them to be determined through a *convention or consensus of the competent* (the "experts" or "wise" (*sophoi*), the abler and persuasively stronger; cf. *Theaetetus*, 169d and 171e ff.) And there is an element of unconventionalistic realism implicit in the issue of who "the competent" are, since their selection is not arbitrary and haphazard, but, rather, is determined by the consideration of who "makes it to the top" in the natural, *phusis*-determined struggle for primacy in the social group or community or profession. An inseparable *mixture* of *nomos* and *phusis* is thus inherent in the idea of a "consensus of the competent," seeing that consensus is conventional but competency has an ineliminable element of realism.

As a sympathetic examination of their position indicates, the Greek Sophists deserve to be credited with a well thought out and coherent overall position far removed from the farrago ascribed to them by many historians of philosophy.

9. CONCLUSION: HOW INNOVATIVE WERE THE GREEK SCEPTICS?

When we look at the matter in doxographic perspective, focussing our attention on the teachings and doctrines at issue, it emerges that the whole of anti-cognitivism of the Greek sceptics—as regards both the nature and the grounds of the position—was substantially anticipated by the Sophists. Effectively the whole story of the Sceptics' negativism regarding the prospects for human knowledge of reality was already part and parcel of Sophistical teaching. But the point at which the Sceptics parted ways from the Sophists was in their view of the *practical implications* that this shared negativism has for the management of our personal and public affairs. And it is questionable whether this departure was for the good. For the Sophists avoided the cognitive nihilism into which the Sceptics were to fall by taking a more robust and hopeful view of the human situation. They did not content themselves with advocating a thought-suspensive life based on mere appearances, but supplemented their epistemological scepticism with a personalistic theory of interest and a political philosophy of consensus via a rhetorically managed persuasive appeal to people's interests.

Insofar as this perspective on the historical position of affairs is right, it has to be acknowledged that as far as cognitive scepticism is concerned, the Greek sceptics, like Columbus later on, "discovered" a land already peopled by others. For in fact that part of Greek Scepticism which holds greatest interest for subsequent philosophizing—the anti-cognitivist teaching that wa its largest and most characteristic component—was substantially anticipated by the Sophists.[31], [32]

NOTES

[1] Recent discussions of Greek Sceptics have been preternaturally reticent about scepticism's debt to the Sophists. Two excellent recent anthologies are cases in point. Malcolm Schoefield et. al. *Doubt and Dogmatism* (Oxford: Clarendon Press, 1980), and Myles Burnyeat, *The Sceptical Tradition* (Berkeley and Los Angeles: University of California Press, 1983).

[2] The best recent treatments of Greek sophistry are W. K. C. Guthrie, *The Sophists* (Cambridge: Cambridge University Press, 1971) and G. B. Kerferd, *The Sophists* (Cambridge: Cambridge University Press, 1981). Also useful are H. D. Rankin, *Sophists, Socratics, and Cynics* (London: Croom Helm, 1983), and Eugène Dupréel, *Les Sophistes* (Neuchatel: Editions de Griffon, 1948). Jean-Paul Dumat, *Les Sophists: Fragments et Temoinages* (Paris, 1969) also provides translation of various relevant texts. The classic source is Hermann Diels and Walther Kranz, *Fragmente der Vorsokratiker*, 2 vols. (Berlin: Wiedmann, 1934 and 1935). The section on the Sophists is translated in Rosamund Kent Sprague (ed.), *The Older Sophists* (Columbia, SC: University of South Carolina Press, 1972).

[3] On the other hand, they owe to Plato their very identity. For he inaugurated the idea of lumping the Sophists together into a single "school" with a collective approach.

[4] On the *tropes* see especially Gisela Striker's contribution to *The Sceptical Tradition* ed. by Myles Burnyeat (*op. cit.*). On Greek scepticism and the important distinctions among its various factions see the illuminating discussion in James Allen, "The Skepticism of Sextus Empiricus," In W. Haase and H. Temporini (eds.), *Rise and Decline of the Roman World*, Pt. II, The Principate (Berlin and New York: DeGruyter, 1990.)

[5] I have for some years been engaged in a campaign to gain acceptance for *apory* (pl. *apories*) as an English counterpart of the Greek *aporia*—an analogy with such English derivatives as *harmony, melody, symphony,* or indeed *analogy* itself.

[6] Compare the dictum attributed by Philostratus to Gorgias (DK 82, 5b): "Victories over the barbarians require hymns of celebration, over the Greeks laments."

[7] On this issue see Striker, *op.cit.*, pp. 59 ff. The infeasibility of achieving knowledge with respect to the phenomenal world was also, of course, a doctrine of Plato's.

[8] So reasoned the more radical sceptics of the school of Pyrrho. The more moderate sceptics who followed Philo did not espouse *epochê* but thought that "the probable" (*to pithanon*) could provide a weaker surrogate for actual knowledge.

[9] Compare W.K.G. Guthrie, *The Sophists*, p. 194.

[10] "If the things thought are not [as such] existent, the existent is not thought." Cf. H. J. Newiger, *Untersuchungen zu Gorgias' Schrift über das Nichtseiende* (Berlin, 1973), pp. 1-8.

[11] Compare Kerferd, *The Sophistic Movement*, p. 95.

[12] See also Sextus Empiricus, *Adv. Math.* VII 65.

[13] Socrates goes on to indicate that some who do not go *quite* so far as Protagoras are willing to say that common opinion makes such things true—i.e., are willing actually to speak of "truth" on these matters. (But see also the divergent reading in Myles Burnyeat's *Theatetus*.)

[14] There are certainly honorable exceptions—preeminently G. B. Kerferd and W. K. C. Guthrie—but a few roses do not make a garden.

[15] "All men do all things in pursuit of these two goals: either seeking some profit or averting some harm" (Gorgias, Frag. 11a (DK); Sprague, p. 58).

[16] Thus Gorgias declares: "It is not in nature for the strong to be thwarted by the weaker, but rather for the weaker to be ruled and led by the strong: for the strong to lead and the weak to follow" (Helen 6, DK II 290). According to the Sophist Lycorphron, the nobility of nobles (*eugeneiai*) consists preeminently in the weight given to their words in discussion. (Aristotle, Frag. 91 ed. Rose, *Aristotles pseudepigraphus*, "On Morality," ed. Ross, p. 57.)

[17] Thus Plato's Socrates thinks that he strikes a telling blow against Protagoras in denying that people and states "get it right" when they agree about what is advantageous (*sumpheron*). (See *Theaetetus*, 172a-b.)

[18] The single point of disagreement between the Pyrrhonians and Protagoras regarding the world's unknowability that Sextus Empiricus notes turns on the latter's speculation that Heracleitean changeability ("the fluidity of matter") is what explains our inability to discern the nature of things. This matter, being nonevident, is something about which sceptics should suspend judgment (*adêlôn ontôn kai hêmin ephektôn, Pyrr. Hyp.*, I, 219). What Sextus seems to be saying is substantially this, that the position is much the same, just its *rationale* is different.

[19] For a vivid picture of this practical part of scepticism see Myles Burnyeat "Can the Sceptic Live this Scepticism?" in Malcolm Schofield et al. (eds.), *Doubt and Dogmatism* (Oxford: Clarendon Press, 1980), pp. 220-53.

[20] When the Socrates of Plato's *Theaetetus* argues (178b ff) against Protagoras that people's opinions (*doxai*) regarding what will prove *beneficial* for them are not equally good (contrast the layman with the physician), nor yet are they equally good even as regards what someone will find pleasant (contrast the experienced cook with the culinary ignoramus), he ignores an important aspect of the Sophistic position. A Leitmotiv running through Plato's *Theaetetus* and the *Republic* is the idea that the experts should play the determinative role in political matters—that even as the physician knows what is best for ill people, so the politically sagacious expert knows what is best for the citizens of the community. By contrast, the Sophists, it seems, were willing to run a distinction here. What's best for people is something that they can most effectively judge for themselves, so on the issue of *ends* democracy is called for. But how to secure what is best requires expertise, so on the issue of *means* elitism is in order.

[21] Plato ascribed to Protagoras, Prodicus, and the Sophists at large a doctrine of "the correctness of names" (Protagoras in *Cratylus* 391c; Prodicus in *ibid*, 384b and *Enthydemus* 277e; the Sophists in *Cratylus* 391b) whose concern was with exactly these issues.

[22] The "noble lie" of *Republic* 414c is a strategem of exactly this sort and shows the deep indebtedness of Plato's Socrates to the Sophists he derides.

[23] Conceding that people's language-encapsulated opinion can be "a most untrustworthy thing" through its incapacity to represent reality adequately (Sprague, p. 60), and that speech can, like a drug, "bewitch the soul with a kind of evil persuasion" (Sprague, p. 53), Gorgias maintained that, like certain potentially dangerous drugs, *logos* can also produce good effects, stimulating courage and causing delight. (On this issue cf. Susan C. Jarrall, *Rereading the Sophists* [Carbondale and Edwardsville: Southern Illinois University Press, 1991], pp. 53 ff.) The powers of speech are a favorite theme of his (cf. *Helen*, 12-14; Sprague, pp. 52-53).

[24] In the *Theaetetus* (172a), Plato's Socrates argues against Protagoras that people's *thinking* something to be advantageous does not mean that it actually *is* advantageous for them. But for the sceptical Sophist this consideration constitutes a point of strength rather than weakness. For the social harmony and interpersonal coordination required in a well-functioning state it suffices that people agree on what they deem to be generally advantageous—the more difficult (and, for the sceptic, intractable) question of what really and truly *is* advantageous for people is something which (mercifully) need not be resolved for *these* purposes.

[25]   Compare Guthrie (p. 201), who invokes the table-turning *peritrophê* argument in his complaint that "presumably he [Cralylus] did not carry consistency so far as to deny himself speech in making the criticism of Heraclitus." On *peritrophê* see Sextus Empiricus, *Adv. Log.*, I, 389 ff.

[26]   Frag 26 DK; Sprague, p. 66.

[27]   "For that by which we reveal [information in discourse] is *logos*, but *logos* is not substance and existing things. Therefore we do not reveal existing things to our neighbors, but *logos* which is something other than substance" (*Gorgias*, Frag. 3 DK; Sprague, p. 46).

[28]   This emphasis on the centrality of human artifice led the Sophists to project a theory of progress and to propound a theory of the teachability of virtue unknown in earlier Greek philosophy—a theme particularly stressed in the work of G. B. Kerferd.

[29]   Cf. *Thrasymachus*, Frag. 8 in DK 85; Sprague, p. 93.

[30]   Henry Adams *The Education of Henry Adams* (Boston: Houghton Mifflin, 1961; reprint of the 1907 edition), p. 451.

[31]   I am grateful to James Allen and to Myles Burnyeat for helpful comments on a draft of this paper.

[32]   This essay is a revised version of a paper presented to a conference on scepticism organized by Professor Ezequiel de Olaso in Buenos Aires in May of 1992 and subsequently published in Spanish in the proceedings of this conference. "La deuda del escepticismo griego con los Sofistas," *Revista Latinomericana de Filosofía*, vol. 19 (1993), pp. 33-57.

Chapter 5

ANAXIMANDER, ARISTOTLE, AND "BURIDAN'S ASS"

> *"In things which are absolutely indifferent
> there can be no choice and consequently no option or will,
> since choice must have some reason or principle."*
> G.W. Leibniz

1. INTRODUCTION

The idea that the reasoned life, although rewarding, is not all that simple is already prominent in the earliest speculations on "wisdom" (*sophia*) out of which philosophy (*philo-sophia*) was to grow. Nor is this surprising. After all, a choice that is *reasoned* is more difficult to arrive at than a choice made haphazardly when, in the blithe manner of Mark Twain's dictum, "you pays your money and you takes your choice." But such reflections lead to the puzzle posed by the question: How is a reasoned choice among fully equivalent alternatives possible? We here confront the problem of *choice without preference*: a reasoned choice must proceed from a reasoned preference, but a reasoned preference among fully equivalent objects is patently impossible.

There are puzzles and puzzles—"idle" ones which can at best amuse a sated imagination, and "profound" ones which can lead the intellect into a deeper apprehension of the nature of things. The puzzle of equivalent choices is of the second kind, seeing that its analysis provides an occasion both for insight into the logic of reasoned choice, and for a better understanding of some important issues in the history of philosophy.

As is generally the case in matters of this sort, it is useful to consider the historical background. In elucidating the substantive philosophical contexts in which the problem of choice without preference has figured, and for which it has been viewed as fundamentally relevant, a historical survey brings to light primarily the three following issues: first, its context in Greek science, originally in cosmological discussions of the earth's place in the physical universe, and ultimately in more general considerations regarding physical symmetries (cf. Axiom 1 of Archimedes' treatise *On Plane Equilibriums*); second, its context in philosophico-theological discussion among the Arabs regarding the possibility of explaining God's actions in ways acceptable to reasoning men; and finally its medieval Scholastic context in ethico-theological discussions of man's freedom of the will.

So much for a preview of the historical aspects of our problem. With regard to the theoretical findings of the analysis, let it suffice here to note in a preliminary way that a study of choice without preference forces upon us a clear recognition of the difference between *reasons* on the one hand and inclining *motives* on the other. We shall see that an indifferent choice must be made (in effect) randomly. Now, when a random selection among indifferent objects is made by me, I do have a reason for my particular selection, namely the fact that it was indicated to me by a random selector. But I have no *preference* or psychological motivation of other sorts to incline me to choose this item instead of its (by hypothesis indifferent) alternatives. Such absence of psychological preference does not entail the impossibility of a rationally justifiable selection. A choice can therefore be vindicated as having been made reasonably even though it cannot be traced back to any psychological foundation. In short, we can have *reasons* for a choice even where there is no inclining *motive*. Thus, despite its seemingly abstruse and esoteric character of the issue, the puzzle of a reasoned choice among fully equivalent alternatives is not lacking in instructiveness from both the theoretical and the historical points of view.

2. THE PROBLEM

Can a reasonable agent choose a course of action, or an object, without a preference? It certainly appears on first view that this question has to be answered negatively. By the very concept of a "reasonable agent," it is requisite that such an individual has *reasons* for his actions. And when a reasonable choice among alternatives is made, this must, it would seem, have to be based upon a *preference* for the object actually chosen *vis à vis* its available alternatives. Where there is no *preference*, it would appear that no *reason* for a selection can exist, so that there apparently cannot be a *reasonable* way of making a choice. This line of reasoning seems to establish the precept: *No reasonable choice without a preference*.

However, despite the surface plausibility of this argument, it cannot be accepted as fully correct. For there is a well-known, indeed notorious counter-example: the dilemma or paradox of Buridan's Ass. This mythical creature is a hypothetical animal, hungry, and positioned midway between essentially identical bundles of hay. There is assumed to be no reason why the animal should have a preference for one of the bundles of hay over the other. Yet it must eat one or the other of them, or else starve. Under these circumstances, the creature will, being reasonable, prefer Having-one-bundle-of-hay to Having-no-bundle-of-hay. It therefore *must choose one* of the bundles. Yet there is, by hypothesis, simply no *reason* for preferring either bundle. It appears to follow that reasonable choice must—somehow—be possible in the absence of preference.

It should at once be noted that the problem of the Identity of Indiscernibles, famous because of its prominent role in the philosophy of Leibniz, has no bearing upon the issue. For what is at stake in cases of choice without preference, such as the example of Buridan's ass, is not there being *no difference* between the objects of choice (i.e., that they be strictly indiscernible), but merely that such differences as do admittedly exist are *either* entirely *irrelevant* to the desirability of these items (as the mint-markings of coins in current circulation have no bearing upon their value or worth), or *else* are simply *unknown* to the chooser. Thus indiscernability is not at issue here, but rather effective indistinguishability *qua* objects of choice—value-symmetry, in short—so that every identifiable reason for desiring one alternative is equally a reason for desiring the others. There is consequently no need for the issue of the identity of indiscernibles to concern us in the present context.

In the main, the problem of choice in the absence of preference is a theoretical, and not a practical problem. Real-life situations rarely confront us with strictly indifferent choices. Such situations do, however, appear to exist. For example, if a person were offered a choice between two fresh dollar bills, the only perceptible difference between which is that of their serial numbers, we would be greatly astonished if this selector could offer us a "reason" for choosing one of them rather than the other which could reasonably be regarded as cogent. While a difference between the bills does indeed exist, it simply does not constitute a valid difference as regards their preferability as objects of choice. And again, when purchasing a stamp at the post office, one is utterly indifferent as to which one on the sheet the agent gives one (for *him*, to be sure this indifference is eliminated by such factors as ease of access, etc., so that the *situation* is not one of indifference). However, though it is the case that indifferent choices are rare, the problem of choice without preference does, nevertheless, have the status of an interesting question in the theory of reasoned choice. And as such it also has—as we shall see—significant philosophical implications and consequences, and as well as a venerable history in philosophic thought.

3. THE HISTORY OF THE PROBLEM OF "BURIDAN'S ASS"

The problem of choice without preference has a long philosophical, and even literary, history. Its most noteworthy parts of which will be sketched in this section. The interest of this historical excursus lies both in the view that it provides of various formulations of our puzzle, and in its indication of the alternative philosophical problem contexts in which it has played a significant role.

Anaximander (ca. 610-ca. 545 BC)

According to a report of Origen, already certain of the early Greek cosmologists had held "that the earth is a celestial object (*meteôron*), supported [in the heavens] by nothing whatsoever, and remaining in its place on account of its equidistance from all."[1] From Aristotle we learn that just this was the position and the line of reasoning of the pre-Socratic philosopher, Anaximander of Miletus:

> There are some who name its [i.e., the earth's] indifference (*homoiotês*) as the cause of its remaining at rest, e.g., among the early philosophers Anaximander. These urge that that which is situated at the centre and is equably related to the extremes has no impulse to move in one direction—either upwards or downwards or sideways—rather than in another; and since it is impossible for it to accomplish movement in opposite directions at once, it necessarily remains at rest.[2]

And this idea was endorsed by Socrates in Plato's *Phaedo*:

> "I am satisfied," he [Socrates] said, "in the first place that if [the earth] is spherical, and located in the middle of the universe, it has no need of air[3] or any other force of that sort to make it impossible for it to fall; it is

sufficient by itself to maintain the symmetry of the universe and the equipoise of the earth itself. A thing which is in equipoise and placed in the midst of something symmetrical will not be able to incline more or less towards any particular direction; being in equilibrium, it will remain motionless."[4]

In the thought of Anaximander, then, that an object "placed in the midst of something symmetrical will not be able to incline more or less towards any particular direction" we have the conceptual origin, the germ as it were, of the problem of Buridan's Ass.[5] But this is only the start, and, a further step was required to reach our actual problem—the move to the concept of a psychological cancellation or balance among opposing motivations of equal strength, to a *psychological equilibrium of motives*, in short. This step was already taken by Aristotle.

Aristotle (384-322 BC)

In criticizing as inadequate the very view we have just considered that the earth is sustained in space through the equipoise of the surrounding heavens, Aristotle contrasts this view with his own theory of *natural place*, to the distinct advantage of this latter theory:

The reason [for the earth's position] is not its impartial relation to the extremes: that could be shared by any other element, but motion towards the center is peculiar to earth.... If ... the place where the earth rests is not its natural place, but the cause of its remaining there is the constraint of its "indifference" (on the analogy of the hair which, stretched strongly but evenly at every point, will not break, or the man who is violently but equally hungry and thirsty, and stands at an equal distance from food and drink, and who therefore must remain where he is), then they [i.e., Anaximander and the other supporters of this view] ought to have inquired into the presence of fire at the extremes.... Fire when placed at the centre is under as much necessity to remain there as earth, for it will be related in the same way to any one of the points on the extremity; but in fact it will leave the centre, and move as we observe it to do, if nothing prevents it, towards the extremity....[6]

Here, in Aristotle's extension of the mechanical equilibrium cases into his example of the man torn between equal attraction to food and drink, the physical theme of an equilibrium of forces was first transformed into a psychological balance of motives.

The sixth century Aristotelian commentator Simplicius offers the following discussion on this passage:

> The Sophists say that if a hair composed of similar parts is strongly stretched and the tension is identical throughout the whole, it would not break. For why would it break in this part rather than that, since the hair is identical in all its parts and the tension is identical? Analogously also in the case of a man who is exceedingly hungry and thirsty, and identically so in both, and identically lacking in food and drink, and for this reason identically motivated. Necessarily, they say, this man remains at rest, being moved to neither alternative. For why should he move to this one first, but not that, inasmuch as his need, and thus his motivation, is identical [on each side].... The solution of such examples of identity is hardly surprising. For it is clear that the hair breaks. Even hypothesizing a fictitious thing with parts thus identical, plainly an identical tension at the ends and the middle is impossible. As to the other example, even if the man were equally distant, thirst would press him more. And if neither this nor that presses more, he will choose whatever he first happens on, as when two pleasant sights lie equally in our view. Whatever happens first we choose first. For identity does not completely obviate the choice, but simply makes the drive [towards one alternative] slower by the diversion of the other.[7]

In his discussion of the choice problem, Simplicius rigidly preserves the psychological character of the example as instancing a psychological equilibrium of motives. Simplicius' proposed solution to the problem does, however, offer, an interesting and original suggestion, viz., that indifferent choices can be resolved on grounds of *convenience*, and in particular, that this can be accomplished by selecting the alternative upon which "we happen first." We shall have occasion to revert to this suggestion below.

Before the definition of the philosophic problem of choice without preference was to attain its ultimate logical sharpness of formulation, it was necessary that the mode of indifference at issue should become transformed from a *psychological* balance among diverse motivations into a strict *logical* indifference: a choice in the face of essentially identical alternatives. This was the step taken by al-Ghazâlî, the Algazel of the Schoolmen, and taken first, it would seem, by him.

Ghazâlî (1058-1111)

In his great work on the *Incoherence of the Philosophers*, the Arabic philosopher-theologian Ghazâlî is concerned, *inter alia*, to defend the orthodox Moslem theological thesis of the createdness of the world against the view maintained by the Arabic Aristotelians that the universe is eternal. One of the reasonings which Ghazâlî is concerned to refute is an argument against the createdness of the world based on a concept of sufficient reason: Why, if the world is the creation of God, did he elect to create it when he did, rather than earlier or later?[8] Speaking, for the moment, on behalf of the (Aristotelian) philosophers, Ghazâlî presses this question home against the supporters of the createdness of the world:

But we philosophers know by the necessity of thought that one thing does not distinguish itself from a similar except by a differentiating principle, for if not, it would be possible that the world should come into existence, having the possibility both of existing and of not existing, and that the side of existence, although it has the same possibility as the side of non-existence, should be differentiated without a differentiating principle. If you answer that the Will of God is the differentiating principle, then one has to inquire what differentiates the will, i.e., the reason why it has been differentiated in such or such a way. And if you answer: One does not inquire after the motives of the Eternal, well, let the world then be eternal, and let us not inquire after its Creator and its cause, since one does not inquire after the motives of the Eternal![9]

In opposing this argument, Ghazâlî proceeds by a closer examination of the concept of *will*, seeking to establish the drastic-seeming remedy of a denial that the concept of a sufficient reason for action is applicable to the supreme being,[10] whose will can of itself constitute a differentiating principle.[11] We must accept the idea of a "mere" will—of a choice made not conditionally because it subserves some other willed purpose, but categorically—simply and solely because its willer would have it so.[12] It is of the essence of will, Ghazâlî argues, that choice without reason be possible. Here the will can provide a substitute for reason out of its own resources: *stet pro ratione voluntas.*[13]

We answer: The world exists, in the way it exists, in its time, with its qualities, and in its space, by the Divine Will and will is a quality which has the faculty of differentiating one thing from another, and if it had not this quality, power in itself would suffice. But, since power is equally related to two contraries and a differentiating principle is needed to differentiate one thing from a similar, it is said that the Eternal possesses besides His power a quality which can differentiate between two similars. And to ask why will differentiates one of two similars is like asking why knowledge must comprehend the knowable, and the answer is that "knowledge" is the term for a quality which has just this nature. And in the same way, "will" is the term for a quality the nature or rather the essence of which is to differentiate one things from another.[14]

Ghazâlî proceeds to illustrate by means of an example that this capacity of differentiating where there is no difference is an essential characteristic power of all will, human as well as divine. This example is the focus of our present interest, and merits quotation in full:

How, then, will you refute those who say that rational proof has led to establishing in God a quality the nature of which is to differentiate between two similar things? And, if the word "will" does not apply, call it by another name, for let us not quibble about words! ... Besides, we do not even with respect to our human will concede that this cannot be imagined. Suppose two similar dates in front of a man who has a strong desire for them, but who is unable to take them both. Surely he will take one of them through a quality in hum the nature of which is to differentiate between two similar things. All the distinguishing qualities you have mentioned, like beauty or nearness or facility in taking, we can assume to be absent, but still the possibility of the taking remains. You can choose between two answers: either you merely say that an equivalence in respect to his desire cannot be imagined—but this is a silly answer, for to assume it is indeed possible—or you say that if an equivalence is assumed, the an will remain for every hungry and perplexed, looking at the dates without taking one of them, and without a power to choose or to will, distinct from his desire. And this again is one of those absurdities which are recognized by the necessity of thought. Everyone, therefore, who studies, in the human and the divine, the real working of the act of choice, must necessarily admit a quality the nature of which is to differentiate between two similar things.[15]

Here for the first time the problem of choice without preference is given its ultimate logical formulation. The examples in explanation of Anaximander's views involve a physical balance through the equilibrium of forces; and in Aristotle's example we have the psychological balance of contrary drives or motivations of equal intensity. Ghazâlî's formulation, however, sharpens the dilemma to its logical edge: it poses the problem of *the possibility of rational choice in the face of essentially identical alternatives.*

By right of historical precedence, then, the problem of Buridan's Ass ought perhaps more appropriately be denominated as that of *Ghazâlî's Dates.* However, it seems likely—in view of the manner in which Ghazâlî introduces the problem into his discussion—that he found it already in current consideration.[16] He employs it as an example admirably suited to support the concept of a "mere" will—inscrutable from the standpoint of reasons and reasonings, capable of effecting differentiation where there is no difference.[17]

Ghazâlî associates himself with the school of Moslem theologians called Ash^carites, after its founder al-Ash^cari. Opposing the rationalistic Mu^ctazilites, the Ash^carites make room for a certain irrationality, or better, non-rationality in matters theological, denying that reason alone is capable of attaining religious truths:

The difference between the Ash^carite and Mu^ctazilite conceptions of God cannot be better expressed than by the following passage which is found twice in Ghazâlî ... and to which by tradition is ascribed the breach between al-Ash^cari and the Mu^ctazilites.

Let us imagine a child and a grown-up in Heaven who both died in the True Faith, but the grown-up has a higher place than the child. And the child will ask God, "Why did you give that man a higher place?" And God will answer, "He has done many good works." Then the child will say, "Why did you let me die so soon that I was prevented from doing good?" God will answer, "I knew that you would grow up a sinner, therefore it was better that you should die a child." Then a cry goes up from the damned in the depths of Hell, "Why, O Lord, did you not let us die before we became sinners?"

Ghazâlî adds to this: "The imponderable decisions of God cannot be weighed by the scales of reason and Mu^{c}tazilism."[18]

Averroes (1126-1198)

In his book on the *Incoherence of the Incoherence*, a detailed critical commentary on Ghazâlî's *Incoherence of the Philosophers*, Averroes undertook to defend the Arabic Aristotelians against Ghazâlî's onslaught. It is worth quoting in full his criticism of Ghazâlî's example of the dates:

> It is assumed that in front of a man there are two dates, similar in every way, and it is supposed that he cannot take them both at the same time. It is supposed that no special attraction need be imagined for him in either of them, and that nevertheless he will of necessity distinguish one of them by taking it. But this is an error. For, when one supposes such a thing, and a willer whom necessity prompts to eat or to take the date, then it is by no means a matter of distinguishing between two similar things when, in this condition, he takes one of the two dates ... whichever of the two dates he may take, his aim will be attained and his desire satisfied. His will attaches itself therefore merely to the distinction between the fact of taking one of them and the fact of leaving them altogether; it attaches itself by no means to the act of taking one definite date and distinguishing this act from leaving the other (that is to say, when it is assumed that the desires for the two are equal); he does not prefer the act of taking the one to the act of taking the other, but he prefers the act of taking one of the two, whichever it may be, and he gives a preference to the act of taking over the act of leaving. This is self evident. For distinguishing one from the other means giving a preference to the one over the other, and one cannot give a preponderance to one of two similar things in so far as it is similar to the other—although in their existence as individuals they are not similar since each of two individuals is different from the other by reason of a quality exclusive to it. If, therefore, we assume that the will attaches itself to that special character of one of them, then it can be imagined that the will attaches to the one rather than the other because of the element of difference existing in both. But then the will does not attach to two similar objects, in so far as they are similar.[19]

Essentially, then, Averroes' position was that: (1) it is necessary to grant the preferability of taking-one-date over against taking-neither-date, but (2) there would be no reasonable way of choosing one particular date were it actually to follow from the hypothesis of the problem that there is no reason for preferring one over the other, however, (3) since there are two distinct dates, they must be *distinguishable* so that there must be some element of difference—at least a difference in *identity*—between them, and the will can and must therefore fix upon such an element of difference as a "reason" for preference. Thus Averroes simply reasserts—in the teeth of Ghazâlî's example—the impossibility of choice without preference. And he resolves the impasse by having a difference of the sort that must inevitably exist provide the "reason" for a choice.[20]

The obvious criticism of Averroes' solution is implicit in the quotation marks that have been put about the word *reason*. For it is assumed in the defining statement of the problem that the differences among the objects are such as to have no rationally valid bearing on the matter of their relative preferability. There therefore is, *by hypothesis*, no legitimacy or validity from the standpoint of reasonableness, in any attempt to base a reasoned preference upon these differences.

4. CHOICE IN THE ABSENCE OF PREFERENCE

The leading idea which underlies the sensible resolution of the Buridan's choice perplex inheres in the similarity of logical structure between the problems (1) of choice in the case of symmetry of *knowledge*, and (2) of choice in the case of symmetry of *preference*. To establish the kinship which obtains here, let us first examine the problem of choice with symmetric knowledge.

Consider the following example, a simple variant of Frank Stockton's problem of the lady and the tiger: A person is offered a choice between two similar boxes. He is told only that one box contains some prize, and that the other is empty. He is not told which is which. Here there is no problem of absence of preference: the person has a clear preference for the treasure-box. The only lack is one of *information*—the choice is to be made in the face of absence of any clue as to the *identity* of this treasure-box. While they may differ in other ways (color, for example), with regard to the crucial question—"Which box is empty and which one holds the prize?"—the available information about the boxes is completely *symmetric*.

This example, then, is an instance of the problem of choice under conditions of symmetric information with respect to a particular preferential issue. How, in such cases, can a *reasonable* person go about making a *rationally defensible* choice?

The sensible answer to this question is in fact simple, well-known, and uncontroversial. For consider the example of the boxes. By the hypothesis which defines the problem, there is no item of information at the disposal of the chooser which could be embraced by him as a *reason* for selecting one box rather than the other. This person therefore simply cannot *reasonably* incline toward one box *vis à vis* the other. And this fact of itself must accordingly characterize the manner of his choice. In short, if rational, he must make his selection in a manner which does not favor one box over against the other: he must make his selection in a *random* manner.

This is a matter susceptible of reasoned demonstration. Assume that the boxes are labeled *A* and *B*. Given that, (by hypothesis) the choice of one box produces a result preferable to the rejection of both, the following three courses of action remain available and are mutually exclusive and exhaustive:

(1) To make the choice in some manner that favors selection of Box *A* rather than Box *B*.

(2) To make the choice in some manner that favors selection of Box *B* rather than Box *A*.

(3) To make the choice by means of a selection process that is wholly impartial as between Box *A* and Box *B*, i.e., to choose *randomly*.

Observe, to begin with, that probabilistic considerations as to expected gain do not enter in at all—on the basis of the available information it is *equally probable* that Box *A* holds the treasure as Box *B*, so that the expected gain with *any* of the three procedures (1)—(3) is precisely the same, viz., one-half the value of the treasure. Thus on the sole grounds of expected gain there is no difference among these alternatives. But from the standpoint of *reasonableness* there is a very significant difference among the selection procedures. For by the defining hypothesis of the problem, there is no known reason for favoring Box *A* as against Box *B*, or conversely. This very fact renders it rationally indefensible to adopt (1) or (2).

Per contra, this symmetry of knowledge *of itself constitutes an entirely valid reason for adopting* (3). This line of reasoning establishes the thesis—pivotal for present purposes—that: *In the case of symmetric knowledge, random choice is the reasonable policy.*

It is be useful to note a corollary of this thesis. When such a problem of choice with symmetric information arises, there is no reason (by the very nature of the problem) why we ought not to regard the *arrival order* in which the choices are given in the formulation or situation of the problem as being purely adventitious, i.e., as a random ordering. The following policy would thus be entirely reasonable and justified: whenever confronted with a choice in the face of symmetric knowledge, to select that alternative which is the first[21] to come to view. (Compare the discussion of Simplicius given above) Such a policy is defensible as entirely reasonable, since under usual circumstances the arrival order can be taken, by the defining hypothesis of the problem, to be a random ordering.

It is important to note that the matter of a *policy* of choice is very important in this context. When I make a choice among symmetrically characterized alternatives, I *can* defend it, reasonably, by saying, "I chose the first mentioned (or the like) alternative, because I *always* choose the first-mentioned (etc.) in these cases."[22] But I cannot (reasonably) defend the choice by saying, "I chose the first mentioned alternative because this seemed to me to be the thing to do *in this case*, though heaven knows what I would do on other occasions."

The adequacy of such selection policies in the face of indifference based on "convenience" is of fundamental importance because this alone averts an infinite regress of random selections in cases of indifferent choice. For if such choice had always to be made by a random device, the following regress would at once ensue: We are to choose between the indifferent alternatives *A* and *B*. We take a random instrument, say a coin, as means of resolution (since, by hypothesis, we must have actual recourse to a randomizing instrument). We must now, however, choose between the alternatives:

(I) To associate *heads* with alternative *A* and *tails* with alternative *B*.

(II) To associate *tails* with alternative *A* and *heads* with alternative *B*.

It is at once, obvious that this is itself an indifferent choice. Thus if the resolution of our initial indifferent choice between *A* and *B* requires use of a random device, we must, first of all resolve another indifferent choice, that between the alternatives (I) and (II), or their analogues. But now if this choice too must be effected by a random device, it is clear that we shall be faced with another, analogous situation of indifferent choice, and so on *ad infinitum*. Only if we recognize that selections in the face of choice without preference can be effected on the basis of selection policies based on "convenience," and do not invariably necessitate actual employment of actual random devices, can this infinite regress of random selections be circumvented.

It should also be noted, however, that a systematic policy of choice such as, for example, invariable selection of the first-occuring alternative is not a *universally* appropriate substitute for selection by actual outright use of a random device or process. Consider, for example, the following situation of choice. A (fair) coin is tossed. *A* tries to guess the outcome: heads or tails. *B* tries to guess *A*'s selection. If *B* guesses correctly, he wins a penny from *A*, if correctly he pays a penny to him. How is *A* to chose his guesses? Clearly, it would be a poor proposition for *A* always to guess heads, even though he is in a position of total ignorance and indifference with regard to the outcome of heads or tails. And the same holds true of any other program of choice, such as always guessing tails, or alternating, or the like. All of these run the risk that *B* can discern the guessing pattern involved, and then capitalize on this information. The only defensible course, in a situation such as this, is to have outright recourse to a random process or device. (This randomizing instrument may, however, be the human mind, since people are presumably capable of making arbitrary selections,with respect to which they can be adequately certain in their own mind that the choice was made haphazardly, and without any "reasons" whatsoever. To be sure, this process is open to the possible intrusion of unrecognized biases, but then so are physical randomizers such as coins. The randomness of any selection process is a matter which, in cases of importance, shall be checked by empirical means.)

Let us now turn from this discussion of choice in the face of symmetric *knowledge* to the problem of symmetric *preference*. It is clear upon careful consideration that the matter of choice without preference—i.e., under conditions of symmetric preference—can actually be subsumed under the topic of symmetric knowledge as a special case. For in a case of strictly symmetric preference (two essentially similar dates, glasses of water, bales of hay, corn, etc.), the knowledge or information at our disposal constrains us to regard the objects of choice as equally desirable, because in the circumstances every possible reason for valuing one applies, *mutatis nomine*, to the other(s). So far as the factor of their value or desirability for us is concerned, our knowledge regarding each object is precisely the same.[23] Problems of choice with symmetric valuation can therefore be regarded as simply a species within the symmetric knowledge genus owing to the equivalence of our relevant information in the symmetric value case.

It thus follows that the device of random selection will also provide the means of resolution appropriate for symmetric preference choices. To test the correctness of this resolution, consider Ghazâlî's example of a man who had the choice between two ostensibly identical dates. Logically, there are three courses of action open to him, with the ensuing reward as indicated.

Course of Action	Reward
(1) To select *neither* date, for lack of a preference	Nothing
(2) To fix upon one of the dates by means of some selection procedure which favors one over the other	One date
(3) To select one of the dates at *random*	One date

It is clear that these three courses of action are mutually exclusive and exhaustive. But a reasonable person cannot opt for (1), because its associated reward is of lesser value than that of its alternatives. Further, the defining hypothesis of the example—viz., that there is no known reason for preferring one date to the other—of itself constitutes a reason for rejecting (2). Random selection is the only means of avoiding favoring one alternative over the other. And just this constitutes a valid reason for adoption of (3).

These considerations, then, serve to establish the proposition that: *Random selection is the rationally appropriate procedure for making choices in the face of symmetric preference*. The concept of random selection provides an answer to the problem of choice without preference which is, demonstrably, its only *reasonable* (i.e., rationally defensible) resolution.

This proposed resolution of the problem of choice without preference is in fact substantially that which was first proposed by Gataker and Bayle as a general means of solution—though in their case without any justifying discussion of the rationale establishing the validity of this solution. Bayle based his suggestion on the fact that when the problem of choice without preference actually arises in real situations—in particular in the instance of court-precedence cases—resolution by change selection is generally regarded as acceptable, and indeed has acquired the status of customary, official mode of resolution.[24]   But of course custom-conformity does not of itself constitute validation but at best supplies some empirical evidence in support of the reasonableness of the proposed resolution.

5. A POSTSCRIPT ON PHILOSOPHICAL ISSUES

In examining the substantive philosophical contexts in which the problem of choice without preference has figured, and for which it has been viewed as fundamentally relevant, our historical survey has brought the three following issues to the fore:

1. Its Greek context in cosmological discussion of the earth's place in the physical universe (Anaximander, Plato, Aristotle).

2. Its Scholastic context in ethico-theological discussion of man's freedom of will (Aquinas, probably Buridan, and others).

3. Its Arabic context in epistemologico-theological discussion of the amenability of God's choices to reason and to human rationalization, i.e., the possibility of explaining God's actions in ways acceptable to reasoning men (Ghazâlî, Averroes).

The entire problem of a choice balanced among indifferent objects originates, historically and conceptually, in an analogy with physical equilibria, such as a body immobile under the pull of opposing forces (see Plato's *Phaedo* 108 E, vice Anaximander), or a balance-bar at rest under the pressure of opposed, but equal weights (embodied in Axiom 1 of Archimedes' *On Plane Equilibriums*).   Here, the issues involved are not properly philosophical, and the definition of the example is still in its embryonic form, dealing either with mechanical equilibrium, or with psychological balance among conflicting motivations of comparable strength. The problem has not yet reached its philosophically pertinent definition as one of selection among *logically* indifferent alternatives, which it achieved only in the middle ages.

It is a common occurrence in the history of philosophical concepts that a purely scientific discovery or idea metamorphoses—through application to a novel setting in a more far-reaching context—into a matter of philosophical concern and significance. And just this happened with Aristotle's psychological analogy in the present case. Only with the Aristotelian commentators (in Islam, Ghazâlî, and Averroes) did the philosophical problem of choice among strictly indifferent objects reach its ultimate *logical* formulation. Genetically, as correctly noted by Reid, the philosophic problem of choice without preference descends from a physical problem-setting, deriving ultimately from analogy with mechanical equilibrium.

With respect to the free-will context, it must be recognized that use of the Buridan example rests upon, and is inextricably embedded in, the scholastic identification of *cause* and *reason*.[25] Once we reject this identification, as indeed we must, the bearing of the example changes. For a situation of choice in which a preferring *reason* for a selection is absent need not now be one in which no *cause* (other than the agency of a "free will") is operative in leading to choice. Thus outside the context of scholastic presuppositions, the example becomes incapable of establishing the immobilization that it claims.

It deserves stress that our problem serves also to highlight the difference between *reasons* and *motives*. When a random selection among indifferent objects is made by me, I do have a *reason* for my particular selection, namely the fact that it was indicated to me by a random selector. But I have no *preference* or psychological motivation of other sorts to incline me to choose this item instead of its (by hypothesis indifferent) alternatives. Such absence of psychological preference does not entail the impossibility of a logically justifiable selection. A choice can, therefore, be logically vindicated as having been made reasonably even though it cannot be traced back to any psychological foundation. In short, we can have *reasons* for a choice even where there is no *motive*.

We come down to the remaining context, the rationalizability of divine choice. Before entering upon a closer consideration of this matter, it is desirable first to take up some other, preliminary observations.

The solution presented in the foregoing section establishes the central role played by *randomness* in the theory of rational choice and decision. A *rational* person must, by the very meaning of the term, fashion his belief and his action intune with the *evidence* at his disposal. In symmetric choice situations, therefore, in which the manifold of reasons—the available ramification—bears identically on every side, he must choose—as has been seen—in a random manner. In such cases, the "reasons" for his choice are independent of any distinguishing characteristic of the object of choice. Here, reasonable choice comes to be possible in the absence of preference only by essentially abdicating the right of choice, in delegating the selection to a random process. Seeing that there simply is *no reasonably defensible way of actually "choosing"* among alternatives in the face of symmetric knowledge. We have either to hand the task of fixing upon a selection over to some random mechanism, by making it contingent upon the outcome of such a device, or else we have to make our selection in accordance with the prescript of some predetermined policy which we can defensibly construe as constituting a random selection process. In either event, we can be said to have "made a *choice*" purely by courtesy. It would be more rigorously correct to say that we have *effected a selection*. In situations of choice without preference, a reasonable person is not condemned to paralysis and inaction. He can and does select, but does so in a random manner, and thus at the price that "his choice" is "his" in only a Pickwickian sense.[26]

Thus in a world in which all things are indifferent, all choices are random, and wisdom and morality will alike come to naught. Just this is the criticism advanced by Cicero against the Stoic teaching that all things of this world should be "indifferent" to the wise man. Cicero writes:

> If we maintained that all things were absolutely indifferent, the whole of life would be thrown into confusion ... and no function or task could be found for wisdom, since there would be absolutely no distinction between the things that pertain to the conduct of life, and no choice need be exercised among them.[27]

Consequently the idea of randomness must play a key part in the theory of rational choice. The concept of randomness which is at issue here is not that of mathematics, as characterized by the criteria which govern the construction of random number of tables. Rather, it is its logical cognate: an alternative is *randomly selected* (in this logical sense) if the selection situation is such that the sum total of the weight of evidence for the selection of the chosen alternative is equal to the weight of evidence for selection of its competing alternatives. (Symmetric information or evidence is a special case of evidence of equal weight.) This concept of randomness as based on evidence is a wholly logical or epistemological concept, which relativizes randomness to knowledge and ignorance.[28]

Another line of consideration is worth noting in this connection. Already Pierre Bayle quite correctly perceived that the problem of choice without preference can take on two forms: (1) selection of one among several (exclusive) alternatives that are essentially identical as regards their desirability-status as objects of possession or realization, i.e., choice without preference among the *objects* involved (the problem of Buridan's Ass), and (2) selection of one among several alternative claimants, whose claims are indivisible and uncompromisable, and whose claims are essentially identical in strength, and must therefore in fairness be treated alike, i.e., choice without preference among the *subjects* involved. Bayle properly recognizes that the device of random selection provides a means of resolution that is entirely appropriate for both cases alike. Random selection, it is clear, constitutes the sole wholly satisfactory manner of resolving exclusive choice between equivalent claims in a wholly fair and unobjectionable manner. Only random, and thus strictly "unreasoned" choice provides an airtight guarantee that there is no answer forthcoming to the question: "Why was this alternative, rather than another, selected?" Random choice thus guarantees that the other alternatives *might just as well* (in the strictest of senses) have been designated. Where there is no way of *predicting* the outcome in advance no charge of preferential treatment can possibly be substantiated. Thus random choice affords the appropriate avenue of resolution for selection-situations in which considerations of fairness leave no other courses of immediate resolution open as acceptable or as defensible.

This consideration has further implications of philosophical import. For one thing, it is surely a *contingent* fact that random processes and devices exist in the world: it is logically feasible to conceive of a possible universe without them. Now the abstract problem of choice without preference is, in its abstract essentials, a theoretical and not a practical problem. It seems curious that the solution of this *theoretical* problem hinges upon the availability of an instrumentality (viz., random choice) whose existence is *contingent*. Surprisingly, it is thus possible to conceive of circumstances (specifically, symmetric choice situations) in which the possibility of rational action depends upon an otherwise wholly extraneous matter of contingent fact (the availability to rational agents of random selection methods). (The availability of random selection policies does however blunt the concept of this consideration.)

Now let us finally return to examining the bearing of the foregoing discussion upon the question—much disputed, alike in medieval Islam, Judaism, and Christianity—as to the reasonableness of God's choices[29]. Here it is—or should be—perfectly clear that as a means of resolving the problem of choice without preference the proposed solution is entirely inapplicable. Orthodox Islamic theology, no less than Christian or Judaic, cannot grant that the concept of random selection has any applicability to the divinity. There can be no chance mechanisms or processes whose outcome is not known to God, nor need He trouble with weights of evidence: in postulating divine omniscience, no possibility is left open for random choice.[30] God's knowledge being complete and timeless, selection cannot be delegated by Him to some contingently future outcome or to some element of serial ordering, such as "the first" (or "the last") alternative.

If follows that the proposed resolution of the problem of choice without preference must be held to apply to the human sphere alone, and not the divine. Only man's ignorance permits him to resolve questions of choice without preference behind the veil of chance.

Once we allow (against Leibniz) the possibility that strictly indifferent choices can arise for the supreme being, we must, I think, be prepared to grant the right to Ghazâlî, against the Arabic Aristotelians. For here a solution is possible only in terms of an inscrutable will, capable of effecting out of its own resources differentiations in the absence of any relevant difference.[31]   It is, accordingly, clear that we must renounce the possibility of human rationalization of divine acts.

The problem of choice without preference was a shrewdly selected example in support of the position maintained by the Islamic theologians in their dispute with the philosophers: this problem does illustrate effectively the thesis of Arabic scholasticism that choices made by the divine intellect may ultimately prove inscrutable in human terms of reference.[32] But in this regard, as in others, medieval Islamic Scholasticism, like the Christian counterpart it so heavily influenced, was itself substantially indebted to its Greek antecedents.[33]

NOTES

1   Origin, *Philosophoumena*, c. 6. My translation.

2   Aristotle, *De caelo*, II 13, 295b10. Tr. by W.K.C. Guthrie in the Loeb Series. Regarding this passage and its bearing on Anaximander see E. Zeller, *Philosophie der Griechen*, vol. I, 7th edition, ed. by W. Nestle (Leipzig, 1923), p. 303, notes.

3   According to Aristotle (*De caelo*, II 13, 294b14), Anaximenes, Anaxgoras and Democritus held that the earth stays in place "owing to the air beneath, like the water in *klepsydrae*."

4   Plato, *Phaedo*, 108 E. Tr. by R.S. Bluck (London, 1955). This reasoning is endorsed also by Parmenides and by Democritus (see Aetios III, 15, 7), who are also reported to have characterized the state resulting from the earth's equidistance from the cosmic extremities as one of *isorropia* (equilibrium: the term used by Pre-Socratics and by Plato in the citation). Again, according to a report of Achilles (*Isagogê*, 4; ed. by V. Arnim, vol. II, p. 555), "The Stoics ... [hold that] the earth will remain in the center, being kept in equilibrium by the pressure of air from all sides. And again, if one takes a body and ties it from all sides with cords and pulls them with precisely equal force, the body will stay and remain in its place, because it is dragged equally from all sides." (I take the reference and the translation from S. Sambursky, *Isis*, vol. 49 [1958], pp. 331-335.) Cp. the "explanation" given in medieval times by eager Christians anxious to refute the supposed miracle that Mohammed's coffin had floated unsupported in mid-air, by claiming that it was made of iron and was supported just midway between two precisely equal magnets.

5   Compare Archimedes' axiom: "I postulate that equal weights at equal distances balance, and equal weights at unequal distances do not balance, but incline towards the weight which is at the greater distance" (*On Plane Equilibriums*, tr. by I. Thomas in *Greek Mathematics* [Loeb], vol. ii, p. 207, Axiom I).

6   Aristotle, *De caelo*, II 13, 295b24. Tr. by W.K.C. Guthrie in Loeb series.

7   *Commentaria in Aristotelem Graeca* (Royal Prussian Academy), vol. VII, *Simplicii in Aristotelis de Caelo Commentaria*, ed. by I.L. Heilberg (Berlin, 1894), pp. 533-534. My translation.

8   "How will you defend yourselves, theologians, against the philosophers, when they ... [say] that times are equivalent so far as the possibility that the Divine Will should attach itself to them is concerned ... ?" Averroes' *Tahâfut al-Tahâfut*, tr.

by S. van den Bergh (London, 1954), vol. I, p. 18. (All questions from this work are drawn from this edition.) Ghazâli's work is quoted *in extenso* in Averroes' commentary thereon, *The Incoherence of the Incoherence*.

[9]   Averroes,*Tahâfut al-Tahâfut*, vol. I. p. 18. Compare R.G. Collingwood's discussion in *The Idea of Nature* (Oxford, 1945): "Unless God had a reason for His choice [to create the world as He did], it was no choice: it was something of which we have no conception whatever, and calling it a choice is merely throwing dust in our own eyes by pretending to equate it with a familiar human activity, the activity of choosing, which we do not in fact conceive it to have resembled. Choice is choice between alternatives, and these alternatives must be distinguishable, or they are not alternatives; moreover one must in some way present itself as more attractive than the other, or it cannot be chosen. [Cp. Averroes and Leibniz below—N.R.] ... To speak of Him as choosing implies either that He chooses for a reason ... or else He chooses for no reason, in which case he does not choose. And the dilemma cannot be evaded by a profession of reverent ignorance. You cannot wriggle out of it by saying that there are mysteries into which you will not pry: that God's ways are past finding out, or (if you prefer one kind of humbug to another) that these are ultimate problems .... Humbug of that kind arises from a kind of pseudo-religiosity .... It is humbug, because it was yourself that began prying into these mysteries. You dragged the name of God into your cosmology because you thought you could conjure with it. You now find you cannot; which proves, not that God is great, but that you are a bad conjurer" (pp. 40-41). Compare Spinoza, who flatly characterizes the "will of God" as "the refuge for ignorance" (*Ethics*, Bk. I, Appendix).

[10]   In Christian theology, this was the position of Duns Scotus: "If it be asked why the divine will is determined rather to one of two incompatables than to the other, I reply: it is foolish (*indisciplinatus*) to seek causes and demonstrations for all things ... there is no cause on account of which the will wills, just as there is no willing to will" (*Opus oxoniensis*, I vii 5, 23-24). My translation is from the Latin cited by C.R.S. Harris in *Duns Scotus* (Oxford, 1927), vol. I, p. 181.

In Jewish theology, this view is espoused by Moses Maimonides: "We remain firm in our belief that the whole Universe was created in accordance with the will of God, and we do not inquire for any other cause or object. Just as we do ask what is the purpose of God's existence so we do not ask what was the object of His will, which is the cause of the existence of all things with their present properties, both those that have been created and those that will be created" (*Guide for the Perplexed*, vol. III, p. 13, tr. by M. Friedländer [American edition, 1946], p. 276).

[11]   In his controversy with Leibniz, Samuel Clarke maintained just this thesis, "Tis very true, that nothing *is*, without a sufficient *reason* it is, and why it is *thus* rather

than *otherwise*. . . . But *sufficient reason* is ofttimes no other, than the *mere Will of God.*" (Second reply, §1.)

[12] This idea is not unfamiliar to readers of the *Arabian Nights* as a characteristic feature of the type of medieval oriental despotism there depicted. When one in authority gives as his "reason" for wanting a thing done that "It must needs be so, there is no help for it," this is to be accepted as constituting a very convincing reason indeed.

[13] See note 18 below.

[14] Averroes, *Tahâfut al-Tahâfut*, vol. I, p. 19.

[15] Averroes, *Tahâfut al-Tahâfut*, vol. I, p. 21. This is Ghazâli's reply to a hypothetical philosopher-opponent who said, "The assumption of a quality the nature of which is to differentiate one things from a similar one is something incomprehensible, say even contradictory, for 'similar' means not to be differentiated, and 'differentiated' means not similar.... If someone who is thirsty has before him two cups of water, similar in everything in respect to his aim, it will not be possible for him to take either of them. No, he can only take the one he thinks more beautiful or lighter or nearer to his right hand, if he is right-handed,or act for some such reason, hidden or known. Without this the differentiation of the one from the other cannot be imagined" (*Ibid.*, p. 19).

[16] He may well have owed it to a Syriac or Arabic commentator on Aristotle, presumably in a gloss on *De Caelo*, 295b10-35, although the Greek commentators do not seem to have modified Aristotle's formulation of the example (cf. the quotation for Simplicius given above and also see C.A. Brandis' edition of the *Scholia in Aristotelem*, published by the Royal Prussian Academy, Vol. 4 [1836], p. 507). Thus Léon Gauthier argues that Ghazâli must have found the example already present in Alfarabi or in Avicenna "because he explicitly states at the end of the first Preamble of the *Tahâfut* that throughout this work, in refuting the doctrines of the Greek philosophers, especially Aristotle and his commentators, he limits his considerations to those ideas taken up and endorsed by their two great Moslem disciples, Alfarabi and Avicenna" ("L'Argument de l'Ane de Buridan et les Philosophes Arabes," *Mélanges René Basset [Publications de l'Institut des Hautes-Études Marocaines*, Vol. X], Paris, 1923, pp. 209-233; see p. 224).

[17] This position was adopted by many (Western) scholastics. Johannes Gerson, for example, says that the will *est sibi frequenter sufficiens causa vel ratio* and that it can choose one thing and reject another in such a manner that *nec exterior alia ratio quarenda est: sic volo, sic jubeo; stat pro ratione voluntas (Opera Omnia*, ed. by M.L.E. Du Pin [Antwerp-Amsterdam, 1706], vol. III, pp. 443-444.) On Gerson's theory of the will see H. Siebeck, "Die Willenslehre bei Duns Scotus und

seinen Nachfolgern," *Zeitschrift für Philosophie und Philosophische Kritik*, vol. 112 (1898), pp. 179-216.

[18] S. van den Bergh, p. x of his Introduction to the *Tahâfut al-Tahâfut*. Compare St. Paul: "Nay but, O man, who art thou that repliest against God? Shall the thing formed say to him that formed it, Why hast thou made me thus? Hath not the potter power over the clay, of the same lump to make one vessel unto honour and another unto dishonour?" (*Romans* 9:20-21). Cp. also Omar Khayyam's *Rubaiyât*.

[19] *Tahâfut al-Tahâfut*, vol. I, pp. 22-23.

[20] In his very valuable footnotes on Averroes' text, S. van den Bergh, the learned translator of the *Tahâfut al-Tahâfut* into English, writes: "Averroes misses the point here completely. Certainly the donkey will take one or the other of the two bundles rather than die, but the question is what determines its taking the one rather than the other. Obviously it will take the one that comes first to hand; only, when there is a complete equivalence of all conditions, this is impossible, and Spinoza says bluntly that the donkey will have to die. As a matter of fact, in such cases a complete equivalence of psychological and physical conditions is never reached; no living body even is strictly symmetrical, and if *per impossible* such an equivalence could be momentarily reached, the world is changing, not static, and the donkey will move and not die" (*Tahâfut al-Tahâfut*, vol. II, p. 20). The point here is twofold: (1) that a complete equilibrium of opposing motivations can never actually be reached, and (2) that even if such an equilibrium, albeit impossible, were to be reached, such a condition would necessarily pass due to an inherent instability. The first of these has been asserted in the present context by numerous writers—Montaigne, Bayle, and Leibniz among others—and we shall return to it below. However, van den Bergh is the first to urge the second thesis: that a psychological equilibrium would be intrinsically unstable, and would become resolved because "the world is changing, not static." However, since physical equilibrium is in theory possible in a changing world, it would seem that a better case must be made out for this thesis.

[21] Or "the last" or "the second" or "the penultimate" etc., etc.

[22] "Why?" "Because this amounts to a random choice." "Why do you choose randomly?" "Because random choice is the only rationally defensible policy in such cases." (Why?—Re-read the foregoing!).

[23] It is clear, then, that this analysis does not apply in the case of the *psychological* dilemma of a balance among diverse motivations of equal force (e.g., hunger and thirst), but obtains solely with respect to the *logical* dilemma of choice among strictly comparable alternatives.

[24] According to a *New York Times* report (Monday, January 12, 1959, p. 6), "chance is the arbiter prescribed by Swedish law for breaking tie votes in Parliament," The report states that "a drawing of lots may decide the fate of a controversial pension plan," but goes on to observe that "legislation by lottery has never yet been necessary on any major issue." Again, when Hawaii was admitted as the fiftieth state of the United States, and two new senators were elected, random devices were used by the Senate to decide which of the two new Hawaiian senators would have seniority (decision by a coin-toss), and which would serve the longer term (decision by card-drawing). See the *New York Times* front-page report of August 25, 1959.

[25] Schopenhauer's monograph on *The Fourfold Root of the Principle of Sufficient Reason* provides an extended critique of this confusion of *logical reason* with real cause.

[26] It should be noted that in games of chance, situations in which *rational* choices of courses of action must be made probabilistically can also arise (when the *optimal* strategy is one which is *mixed*). See any text or treatise on the mathematical Theory of Games.

[27] Cirero, *De Finibus*, Bk. III, § 50. I quote H. Rackham's translation in the Loeb series.

[28] Cf. Hume's thesis that "though there be no such thing as *chance* in the world; our ignorance of the real causes of any event has the same influence on the understanding, and begets a like species of belief or opinion" (*Enquiry*, Bk. VI, first sentence). For further explanation of the concept of evidence and of measures of evidential weight, the reader is referred to the writer's paper on "A Theory of Evidence," *Philosophy of Science*, vol. 25 (1958), pp. 83-94.

[29] The significance of this discussion does not hinge on the issue of God's existence. Its bearing is entirerly hypothetical: if there were a God along the traditional lines how would he function?

[30] In the "Introduction" to the *Analogy*, Bishop Butler writes: "Probable evidence, in its very nature, affords but an imperfect kind of information; and is to be considered as relative only to beings of limited capacities. For nothing which is the possible object of knowledge, whether past, present,or future, can be probable to an infinite intelligence; since it cannot be discerned absolutely as it is in itself, certainly true or certainly false. But to us, probability is the very guide of life."

[31] Ghazâli makes the point (*Tahâfut all-Tahâfut*, vol. I, pp. 18-19) that it is senseless to speak of God making choices by chance, for instead of saying, "God chose to do so-and-so in a chance manner" one might instead just a well say, "So-and-so happened by chance."

32   Jonathan Edwards offers the following remarks: "If, in the instance of the two spheres, perfectly alike, it be supposed possible that God might have made them in a contrary position: that which is made at the right hand, being made at the left: then I ask, whether it is not evidently equally possible, if God had made but one of them, and that in the place of the right-hand globe, that he might have made that numerically different from what it is, and numerically different from what he did make it; though perfectly alike, and in the same place . . . .? Namely, whether he might not have made it numerically the same with that which he has now made at the left hand, and so have left that which is now crated at the right hand, in a state of non-existence?   And if so, whether it would not have been possible to have made one in that place, perfectly like these, and yet numerically different from both?   And let it be considered, whether from this notion of a numerical difference in bodies, perfectly alike. . . . it will not follow, that there is an infinite number of numerically different possible bodies, perfectly alike, among which God chooses, by a self-determining power, when he sets about to make bodies." (*A Careful and Strict Enquiry into the Modern Prevailing Notions of that Freedom of Will which is supposed to be Essential to Moral Agency, Virtue and Vice, Reward and Punishment, Praise and Blame* [Boston, 1754], pt. II, sect. xii, subsect. i. Quoted from A.N. Prior, *Past, Present and Future* [Oxford, 1967], pp. 141-142.)

33   This essay is an abbreviated version of an article entitled "Choice Without Preference: The Problem of 'Buridan's Ass'," originally published in *Kantstudien*, vol. 51 (1959/1960), pp. 142-175.

Chapter 6

ARISTOTLE ON ECTHESIS AND APODEICTIC SYLLOGISMS

1. INTRODUCTION

Virtually all modal logicians after Aristotle have been troubled by his insistence that, given a valid *first figure* categorical syllogism (of the purely assertoric type *XXX*)

> Major premiss
> Minor premiss
> Conclusion

the corresponding modal syllogism of type LXL, inferring the necessity of the conclusion from that of the major alone

> Necessarily: Major premiss
> Minor premiss
> Necessarily: Conclusion

must also be valid. (Here *X* indicates the assertoric and *L* the apodeictic mode.) Accordingly, the corresponding *LLL* syllogism must, of course, also be valid *a fortiori*, while the corresponding *XLL* syllogism will—so Aristotle has it—be invalid. Despite extensive consideration of the problems, a convincing rationale for Aristotle's theory has yet to be provided.[1] The aim of the present discussion is to propose a suggestion along these lines that may, perhaps, serve to fill this gap.

The leading idea of the present proposal is that given two Aristotelian syllogistic terms α and β it is possible to define yet another term [αβ] to represent the β subspecies of α. As will be seen below, these *bracketed terms* represent a version of Aristotle's process of *ecthesis*—"selecting out" a part of the range of a syllogistic term that is seen as representing a subspecies of a particular sort.   On this basis, the [αβ]'s are to be"specifically those α's that are by nature β's"; they are those α's which *must* be β's in virtue of their being α's (i.e. by conditional or relative necessitation).

The essential point regarding this special term, one that is central for present purposes, is that it is such as to validate automatically the modality-strengthening inference:

$$\frac{A\alpha\beta}{LA\alpha[\alpha\beta]}$$

Intuitively, if all α's are β's, then all α's must necessarily be [αβ]'s—that is, they will necessarily belong to the β-oriented subspecies of α (consisting of α's that are β's by virtue of being α's). Correspondingly, we would also have the inference:

$$\frac{I\alpha\beta}{LI\alpha[\alpha\beta]}$$

Intuitively, if some α's are β's, then all of *these* α's will of necessity be [αβ]'s so that, in consequence, some α's will of necessity be [αβ]'s.

The bracketed ecthesis-terms are *designed* to validate these two inferences. In view of the proposed construction of bracketed terms, we shall automatically have it that from $A[\alpha\beta]\gamma$ or $I[\alpha\beta]\gamma$ one can infer $I\alpha\gamma$. Moreover, from $E[\alpha\beta]\gamma$ or $O[\alpha\beta]\gamma$ one can infer $O\alpha\gamma$. Finally, from $A\alpha\beta$ we can infer $A[\gamma\alpha]\beta$, and from $E\alpha\beta$ we can infer $E[\gamma\alpha]\beta$ (since what holds for all/none of the α's will hold for all/none of the α-oriented subspecies of some other γ).

These bracketed terms provide the building blocks from which an interpretation of Aristotle's spodeictic syllogisms can be constructed. For once they are introduced, it becomes an interesting and significant result that the apodeictic sector of the Aristotelian modal syllogistic follows *in toto* as a natural consequence. Let us see how this works out.

2. THE TECHNICAL SITUATION

The notation and terminology used here will be as in Storrs McCall's *Aristotle's Modal Syllogisms*, except for the additional use of term-bracketing.

Moreover, an (unproblematic) axiomatization of the assertoric moods *XXX*—and correspondingly of the apodeictic moods *LLL*—will be assumed.

To extend this basis to include all the apodeictic moods approved by Aristotle, we shall adopt the following rules with respect to *bracketed terms* (as forestated in the previous discussion):

Group 1: Modal Inferences of Type *X* to *L*

    I. *C Aab LAa*[*ab*]

    II. *C Iab LIa*[*ab*]

These two principles inhere in the nature of the term-bracketing process. Moreover, we shall also have:

Group 2: Modal Inferences of Type *L* to *L*

    III. *C LAab LA[ca]*b

    IV. *C LEab LE*[*ca*]b

These latter two principles may be taken to follow from their L-denuded counterparts.

These four rules together with the laws of conversion and of modal conversion straightforwardly yield all the apodeictic moods. To show that all the valid apodeictic moods are derivable on this basis, we shall establish all of those of the first figure:

Barbara *LXL*:	1.	*LAbc*	hyp
	2.	*Aab*	hyp
	3.	*LAa*[*ab*]	2, I
	4.	*LA*[*ab*]*c*	1, III
	5.	*LAac*	3, 4, Barbara *LLL*
Celarent *LXL*:	1.	*LAbc*	hyp
	2.	*Aab*	hyp
	3.	*LAa*[*ab*]	2, I
	4.	*LE*[*ab*]*c*	1, IV

| | | 5. | LEac | 3, 4, Celarent LLL |

Darii LXL:

1.	LAbc	hyp
2.	Iab	hyp
3.	$LI[ab]$	2, II
4.	$LA[ab]$c	1, III
5.	LIac	3, 4, Darii LLL

Ferio LXL:

1.	LEbc	hyp
2.	Iab	hyp
3.	$LI[ab]$	2, II
4.	$LE[ab]$c	1, IV
5.	LOac	3, 4, Ferio LLL

It should be observed that all the derivations follow a perfectly uniform plan, viz., the use of bracketed terms to obtain (using I/II) a modalization from the assertoric minor premiss, whereupon the bracketed term at issue in this minor can be subsumed as a special case under the apodeictic major (using III/IV).[2]

The adequacy of any formalization of Aristotle's theory of modal syllogisms depends not only on having the right theorems but also on lacking the wrong ones (and this is where the well-known treatment of Lukasiewicz failed badly). An important test case is that the theory will accept Barbara LXL but omit Barbara XLL. We are safe on the first count; how do we fare on the second? Let us attempt to prove Barbara XLL:

Barbara XLL:

1.	Abc	hyp
2.	LAab	hyp
•		
•		
•		
n.	LAac	?

Clearly LAac is unavailable without the introduction of bracketed terms because no otherwise available inference principle yields an LA conclusion without two LA premisses. So let us see what bracketed terms can do. Applying rule I to premiss 1 will yield LAb[bc]. This together with premiss 2 gives us LAa[bc]—by Barbara LLL. But now we are unable to proceed further; we simply cannot infer *LAac* from *LAa*[*bc*].[3] And since this is our only method of attack, Barbara *XLL* cannot be proven.

The remaining first-figure syllogisms will also be blocked for the type *XLL* on analogous grounds. In general, it should be noted that those first-figure *XLL* syllogisms are excluded through two principles:

(1) Disallowing the inference of any L-qualified proposition from a negative assertoric premiss.

(2) Disallowing immediate (i.e. single-premissed) inferences that eliminate [ ] -bracketed terms.

Thus once appropriate restrictions (of a rather plausible sort) are postulated for inferences involving bracketed terms, none of the apodeictic syllogisms Aristotle regards as illicit will be forthcoming through this extended machinery.

This perspective may help to explain Aristotle's silence regarding the validity of *LA*αα. If we are to avert *C A*αβ *LA*αβ (which is crucial), then, given our machinery, we are also committed to rejecting *LA*αα. This may be seen as follows:

1.	*Aab*	hypothesis
2.	*LAa*[*ab*]	1, I
3.	*LAbb*	by the thesis at issue
4.	*LA*[*ab*]*b*	3, III
5.	*LAab*	2, 4, Barbara *LLL*

This serves to motivate the rejection of *LA*αα. And one can perhaps explain Aristotle's lack of explicitness here by observing that if one must reject LAαα, one might well prefer doing so quietly. But, of course, if one is enough of an essentialist, it would seem only natural to take the view that among all the α's some should be α's of necessity but others merely by accident, so that *LA*αα would not be acceptable.

It warrants note that while the Aristotelian modal syllogistic rejects the thesis *LA*αα, the cognate thesis *LA*α[αα] is readily demonstrable:

1.	Aαα	thesis
2.	LAα[αα]	1, I

The α's may not necessarily have to be α's simpliciter, but they will necessarily have to belong to the α-oriented subspecies of the α's.

3. SCIENTIFIC DEMONSTRATION

The deductions given above for the valid first-figure syllogisms of type *XLX* enable us to clear up one of the puzzles of Aristotle-interpretation: the discord between the theory of apodeictic inference presented in *Prior Analytics* and that presented in *Posterior Analytics.*

Aristotle's theory of modal syllogisms has its developmental and conceptual roots in Aristotle's concept of demonstration. To understand the role and nature of the Aristotelian theory of modal syllogisms generally, and of apodeictic syllogisms in particular, we are thus will be advised to look to his concept of scientific reasoning in *Posterior Analytics,* for it is here that we learn clearly and explicitly how Aristotle conceives of the job and function of apodeictic reasoning. The following passages (quoted from the Oxford translation of Aristotle's works) should prove sufficient for our present purposes.

By demonstration I mean a syllogism production of scientific knowledge, a syllogism, that is, the grasp of which is *eo ipso* such knowledge. Assuming then that my thesis as to the nature of scientific knowing is correct, the premisses of demonstrated knowledge must be true, primary, immediate, better known than and prior to the conclusion, which is further related to them as effect to cause. Unless these conditions are satisfied, the basic truths [of a demonstration] will not be "appropriate" to the conclusion (71b17-24.)

Since the object of pure scientific knowledge cannot be other than it is, the truth obtained by demonstrative knowledge will be necessary. And since demonstrative knowledge is only present when we have a demonstration, it follows that demonstration is an inference from necessary premisses. (73a20-24.)

Demonstrative knowledge must rest on necessary basic truths; for the object of scientific knowledge [i.e., that which is known by demonstration] cannot be other than it is. Now attributes attaching essentially to their subjects attach necessarily to them. . . . It follows from his that the premisses of the demonstrative syllogism must be connections essential in the sense explained. . . . We must either state the case thus, or else premise that the conclusion of demonstration is necessary and that a demonstrated conclusion cannot be other than it is, and then infer that the conclusion must be developed from necessary premisses. For though you may reason from true premisses without demonstrating, yet if your premisses are necessary you will assuredly demonstrate—in such necessity you have at once a distinctive character of demonstration. That demonstration proceeds from necessary premisses is also indicated by the fact that the objection we raise against a professed demonstration. That demonstration proceeds from necessary premisses is also indicated by the fact that the objection we raise against a professed demonstration is that a premiss of it is not a necessary truth. . . . A further proof that the conclusion must be developed from necessary premisses is as follows. Where demonstration is possible, one who can give no account which includes the cause has no scientific knowledge. If, then, we suppose a syllogism in which , though A necessarily inheres in C, yet B, the middle term of the demonstration, is not necessarily connected with A and C, then the man who argues thus has no reasoned knowledge of the conclusion, since this conclusion does not owe its necessity to the middle term; for though the conclusion is necessary, the mediating link is a contingent fact. . . . To sum up, then: demonstrative knowledge must be knowledge of a necessary nexus, and therefore must clearly be obtained through a necessary middle term; otherwise its possessor will know neither the cause nor the fact that this conclusion is a necessary connection. (74b5-75a15.)

Note that here—as everywhere—in *Anal. Post.* Aristotle adopts the view that a syllogistic result is necessary only when *both* premisses are necessary. No statement could be more sharply explicit than the following: "All demonstrative reasoning proceeds from necessary of general premisses, the conclusion being necessary if the premisses are necessary and general if the premisses are general." (*Anal. Post.*, 87b23-25.) But this, of course, is a view he does not espouse in *Anal Pr.*, holding there that it suffices (with first-figure syllogisms) for the major premise alone to be necessary.

From our present perspective, however, it becomes easy to see how the discrepancy at issue between *Prior* and *Posterior Analytics* can be resolved. For in all cases, the reasoning at issue in establishing the valid first-figure *LXL* syllogism proceeded by (1) making an *immediate* inference on the assertoric premiss to transform it into a necessary premiss (viz., one with a bracketed term), and from there (2) deriving the desired apodeictic conclusion from an *LLL*-syllogism.   In short, *the only SYLLOGISTIC inference operative in the course of demonstration is indeed of the all-premisses-necessary type.*   In effect, the ultimate justification of an apodeictic inference with an assertoric premiss lies in our capacity to subsume the argument at issue within the framework of a "scientific" syllogism of strictly necessitarian proportions.

The fundamental fact is thus that the "scientific syllogism" of our demonstrative reasoning *must* have necessary premisses. To be sure, apodeictic conclusions can also be established in certain suitable cases where merely assertoric premisses occur. But even here the basis of necessity is in the final analysis mediated by and realized through a genuine scientific demonstration—one that in *altogether* necessary. Once the matter is seen in this light we obtain a plausible reconciliation between the seemingly conflicting Aristotelian views that a scientifically demonstrative inference must proceed from necessary premisses, and yet that an apodeicitic conclusion can be obtained when as assertoric premiss is present.

4. ECTHESIS

Aristotle does not give proofs for Baroco *LLL* and Bocardo *LLL* but merely outlines how they are to proceed (*Anal. Pr.*, I. 8, 30a6)—in both cases by means of ecthesis. This process—which Aristotle leaves somewhat mysterious—is (so we shall suppose) to be construed along the following lines:

(1) Nonmodal ecthesis

$$\frac{I\alpha\beta}{(\exists\gamma)(K\,A\gamma\alpha\;A\gamma\beta)} \qquad \frac{O\alpha\beta}{(\exists\gamma)(K\,A\gamma\alpha\;E\gamma\beta)}$$

This construal on non-modal ecthesis coincides entirely with that of Patzig.[4]

(2) Modal ecthesis

$$\frac{L I\alpha\beta}{(\exists\gamma)(K\,LA[\alpha\gamma]\alpha\;LA[\alpha\gamma]\beta)} \qquad \frac{L O\alpha\beta}{(\exists\gamma)K\,LA[\alpha\gamma]\alpha\;LE[\alpha\gamma]\beta}$$

Ecthesis, thus conceived, is a process for inferring universal categorical propositions from particulars—albeit only *sub rational generalitatis*, as indicated by the use of existential quantifiers.[5] This central feature of the modal case is its recourse to bracketed terms as introduced above.

Let us examine the argument for Baroco *LLL* as Ross presents it. According to Ross (*op. cit.*, p. 317) the proof goes as follows: assume that all *B* is necessarily *A* and that some *C* is necessarily not *A*. Take some species of *C* (say *D*) that is necessarily not *A*. Then all *B* is necessarily *A*, all *D* is necessarily not *A*, therefore all *D* is necessarily not *B* (by Camestres *LLL*). Therefore some *C* is necessarily not *B*. The reasoning may thus be formulated as follows:

1. *LAba*   hyp
2. *LOca*   hyp
3. *(∃d)LE[cd]a* from ecthesis on 2
4. *(∃d)LE[cd]b* 1, 3, Camestres LLL
5. *LOcb*   4

Next consider the argument for Bocardo *LLL*. Ross (*ibid.*) construes the argument as follows: assume that some C is necessarily not A and that all C is necessarily B. Take a species of C (say D) which is necessarily not A. Then all D is necessarily not A, all D is necessarily B, therefore some B is necessarily not A (by Felapton LLL). The reasoning is thus as follows:

1. *LOca*   hyp
2. *LAcb*   hyp
3. *(∃d)LE[cd]a* ecthesis on 1
4. *(∀d)LA[dc]b* 2
5. *LOba*   3, 4, Felapton *LLL*

The use of bracketed terms to explicate modal ecthesis along the lines indicated above thus provides a straightforward way to systematize the Aristotelian justification of certain apodeictic syllogisms.

One further point warrants notice. Suppose that we have a concrete case of the situation:

Major (Law): All *b* is necessarily *c* (*LAbc*)

Minor (Special Case): All *a* is *b* (*Aab*)

We can proceed as follows. We use the considerations adduced above to establish *in abstracto* the *existence* of a mediating term x (viz., $[ab]$) such that:

$LAax$

$LAxc$

and now proceed by a strictly "scientific syllogism" (i.e., an L-premissed one) to demonstrate the conclusion:

$LAac$

But, of course, quantifiers are not available for use in Aristotle's syllogistic. To carry out the demonstrative argument in its natural habitat one would need to *find* the specific middle term whose existence the abstract considerations guarantee. Just this consideration serves to provide a justificatory rationale for Aristotle's construction of the provision of scientific explanations in terms of the search for a middle term and for his assimilation of this search for the middle to the problem of identifying causes. Let us examine this aspect of the situation more closely

5. CONCLUSION

The use of bracketed terms in ecthesis-involving reasonings allows us "to do the impossible" in Aristotelian logic—albeit in a perfectly legitimate way. In the assertoric case we move from a particular to a universal proposition:

$$\frac{LI\alpha\beta}{(\exists\gamma)LA[\alpha\gamma]\beta}$$

And in the modal case we move from an assertoric to an spodeictic proposition:

$$\frac{A\alpha\beta}{LA\alpha[\alpha\beta]}$$

In both cases the bracketing operator enables us to "select" from among all the α's those which—given that a certain relationship holds between the α's and β's—bear any more stringent relationship to the β's than the α's in general do.

In particular, the modal case deserves further comment. It is crucial that the particularized relation the premiss lays down between α and β (their I-linkage) is necessary, otherwise the conclusion would clearly not be forthcoming. Thus *perception*—which can establish particular linkages *de facto* but not necessarily—cannot provide scientific knowledge.[6] Chance conjunctions in general cannot in the very nature of things be subject to demonstrations on necessity.[7]

That nonmodal ecthesis is a logically warranted (indeed virtually trivial) process can be seen along the following lines:

1. Assume by way of hypothesis that: Some *a* is *b* (*I*ab)

2. Let $a_1, a_2, \ldots$ be specifically those *a*'s that are *b*'s and let us designate the group of these a_i, the "*a*'s at issue," as *x*.

3. Then all these *x* are *a*'s (by the definition of *x*) and moreover all *x* are *b*'s

Thus between the "*a*'s at issue," viz., $x_1, x_2, \ldots$, and *b* we have inserted a "middle term" (*x*) in such a way that (1) all the "*a*'s at issue" are *x*'s (and conversely) and (2) All *x*'s are *b*'s.

In the nonmodal case, we have accomplished this insertion of a mediating term in a logically trivial way. But in the modal case, when *some a is necessarily b* the issue of inserting an intermediate *x* such that both *All the a's at issue are x* and *All x is necessarily b* is not trivial at all. For whereas the motivation of the first of the two inferences under consideration is essentially a matter of pure logic that of the second is at bottom not logical, but metaphysical. If some *a*'s are necessarily *b*'s then—so the inference has it—there must be some *a*-delimitative species, the [*ac*]'s *all* of which are necessarily *b*'s. If some metals are necessarily magnet-attracted then there must be a type of metal (e.g. iron) all of which is necessarily magnet-attracted. The governing intuition here operative lies deep in the philosophy of nature: Whenever *a*'s are such that some of them must be *b*'s, then this fact is capable of *rationalization*, i.e., there must in principle be a *natural kind* of *a*'s that are necessarily (essentially, lawfully) *b*'s. If some trees are deciduous then these will have to be some species of trees (viz. elms) that are by nature (i.e. necessarily) deciduous.

A precursor version of the principle of causality is at work here: If some "humans exposed to a certain virus" are in (the naturally necessitated course of things) "humans who contract a certain disease" but some are not, then there must be some *characteristic* present within the former group in virtue of which those of its members exhibiting the characteristic *must all* contract the disease if exposed to it. To explain that some a's have of necessity to be b's we must find a naturally constituted species of the a's all the members of which are necessarily b's.[8] Thus given "Some a's are of necessity b's," it follows from the requisites of explanatory rationalization that for some species c of the a's we have "all c's are necessarily b's." But, of course, what we have here is essentially not a principle of logic but a metaphysical principle of extraordinary rationalization. At this precise juncture, the logic of the matter is applied rather than pure—fusing with the theory of scientific explanation presented in *Posterior Analytics*.

From this standpoint, then , the principle of modal ecthesis

$$\frac{LI\alpha\beta}{(\exists\gamma)K\ LA[\alpha\gamma]\ LA[\alpha\gamma]\beta}$$

is based upon metaphysical rather than strictly logical considerations. This principle underwrites the equivalence:

$$LI\alpha\beta \text{ if and only if } (\exists\gamma)LA[\alpha\gamma]\beta$$

This, in effect, is a "generalization principle for necessary connection." It stipulates that whenever a necessary connection exists between two natural groups α and β the matter cannot rest there. There must be—somehow, no matter how well concealed— a *universal* necessary relationship from which this particular case derives and in which it inheres. There can be no particular necessity as such: necessity, whenever encountered, is always a specific instance of a *universal* necessity. It is thus easy to see the basis for Aristotle's policy (in *Posterior Analytics* and elsewhere) of assimilating necessity to universality, This perspective highlights Aristotle's fundamental position that science, since it deals with the necessary, cannot but deal with the universal as well. The irreducibly particular—the accidental—lies wholly outside the sphere of scientific rationalization.

Insofar as this view of the matter has merit, it goes to indicate that the fundamental motivation of Aristotle's modal syllogistic is heavily indebted to metaphysical rather than strictly logical considerations. But be this as it may, it is, in any case, significant that by introducing such an ecthesis-related specification of terms, the apodeictic sector of Aristotle's modal syllogistic is capable of complete and straightforward systematization. The crux is that Aristotle's doctrine of scientific syllogisms, his theory of modal ecthesis, and his conception of natural categories are bound together in one tight and indissoluble knot—all linked to a doctrine of organic speciation that cuts loose from its biological ties to diffuse itself throughout his metaphysic.[9]

NOTES

1   For an overview of reconstructive efforts, together with references to the literature, see Storrs McCall, *Aristotle's Modal Syllogisms* (Amsterdam, 1963) and Nicholas Rescher, "Aristotle's Theory of Modal Syllogisms and Its Interpretation, " in *Essays in Philosophical Analysis* (Pittsburgh, 1969), pp. 33-60. For the general background of the Aristotelian syllogistic see Günther Patzig, *Aristotle's Theory of the Syllogism* (Dordrecht, 1968).

2   This substantiates the author's idea (*op. cit.*, pp. 53-55), that a leading intuition of Aristotle's spodeictic syllogistic is that of a special case falling under a necessary rule. And this line of thought itself indicates that Aristotle espouses the validity of Barbara LXL not on grounds of abstract formal logic, but on grounds of *applied* logic, on *epistemological* grounds. What he has in mind is the application of modal syllogisms within the framework of the theory of scientific inference along the lines of his own conceptions. We must recognize that it is Aristotle's concept that in truly scientific reasoning the relationship of major to minor premiss is governed by the proportion:

major premiss : minor premiss :: general rule : special rule

3   This inference would be manageable only if we had $LA[bc]c$, which is unattainable in the circumstances.

4   Cf. Günther Patzig, *Aristotle's Theory of the Syllogism* (Dordrecht, 1968), pp. 156-168. In support of his interpretation of nonmodal ecthesis, Patzig cites *Anal. Pr.*, i.28, 43b43-44a2 and 44a9-11, which appears to be a statement of the equivalence of the premisses and their respective conclusions in (10. Aristotle's observations at *An. pr.*, i 6,28a22-26, are simply a *statement* of the inverse form of the affirmative case on nonmodal ecthesis, rather than representing—as W.D. Ross complains—an attempt at "merely proving one third-figure syllogism by means of another which is no more obviously valid." W.D. Ross, *Aristotle's prior and Posterior Analytics* (Oxford, 1949), p. 32.

5   The inverse inferences (closely akin to Darapti and Felapton), are, of course also valid, so that we are, in effect, dealing with equivalences.

6   Cf. *Anal. Post.*, I, 31.

7   *Ibid.*

8 The idea is closely analogous with the Kantian "generalization principle" of modern ethics, i.e., the thesis that if some certain men are obligated (or entitled) to do something, then this must be so because they belong to some identifiable group *all* of whose members are obligated (or entitled) to do so.

9 This essay was originally published in *The Review of Metaphysics*, vol. 24 (1971), pp. 678-689. It incorporates work done in collaboration with Dr. Zane Parks.

About the Author

Born in Germany in 1928, Nicholas Rescher is University Professor of Philosophy at the University of Pittsburgh where he is also Co-Chair of the Center for Philosophy of Science. He earned his doctorate at Princeton in 1951 in two year while still at the age of twenty-two—a record for Princeton's Department of Philosophy. He has served as a President of the American Philosophical Association, of the American Catholic Philosophy Association, of the American G. W. Leibniz Society, and of the C. S. Peirce Society and is currently president of the American Metaphysical Society. An honorary member of Corpus Christi College, Oxford, he has been elected to membership in the European Academy of Arts and Sciences (Academia Europaea), the Institut International de Philosophie, and several other learned academies. Having held visiting lectureships at Oxford, Constance, Salamanca, Munich, and Marburg, he has been awarded fellowships by the Ford, Guggenheim, and National Science Foundations. Author of some hundred books ranging over many areas of philosophy, over a dozen of them translated into other languages, he is the recipient of six honorary degrees from universities on three continents, and was awarded the Alexander von Humboldt Prize for Humanistic Scholarship in 1984.

Nicholas.Rescher@ontosverlag

Nicolas Rescher

Value Matters

Studies in Axiology

Series: Practical Philosophy Vol. 8
Edited by Heinrich Ganthaler, Neil Roughley,
Peter Schaber, Herlinde Pauer-Studer
140 pp., Hardcover EUR 58,00
ISBN 3-937202-67-6

This is a study of key issues in value theory, setting out a case for regarding evaluation as a rational and objective enterprise. The principal issues dealt with include the purposive rationale of evaluation, the modus operandi of value reasoning, the fallacies that can arise here, and the role of values in the larger context of philosophical deliberation. A special feature of the book is its defence of absolute values in the face of widespread contemporary antagonism to this idea.

Michel Weber (ed.)

After Whitehead

Rescher on Process Metaphysics

Series: Process Thought, Vol. 1
Edited by Nicholas Rescher • Johanna Seibt
Michel Weber
Advisory Board: Mark Bickard • Jaime Nubiola ·
Roberto Poli
ISBN 3-937202-49-8
339 pp., Hardcover, EUR 89,00

When Rescher's *Process Metaphysics* (1996) was published, it was widely acclaimed as a major step towards the academic recognition of a "mode of thought" that has otherwise been confined within sharp scholarly boundaries. Of course it is not an easy book: despite its stylistic clarity, it remains the complex outcome of a life's work in most areas of philosophy.

The goal of the present volume is to systematically unfold the vices and virtues of *Process Metaphysics*, and thereby to specify the contemporary state of affairs in process thought. To do so, the editor has gathered one focused contribution per chapter, each paper addressing specifically and explicitly its assigned chapter and seeking to promote a dialogue with Rescher. In addition, the volume features Rescher's replies to the papers.

"Whenever Nicholas Rescher writes, philosophers take note. This volume bears witness to that fact. Its essays not only engage Rescher's wrestling with Alfred North Whitehead and process metaphysics in helpful ways but also make distinctive and instructive contributions of their own. This book advances the development of an important and lively philosophical tradition".

John K. Roth, Edward J. Sexton Professor of Philosophy and Director of The Center for the Study of the Holocaust, Genocide, and Human Rights, Claremont McKenna College, USA.

ontos verlag

Frankfurt I Paris I Ebikon I Lancaster I New Brunswick

P.O. Box 15 41
63133 Heusenstamm bei Frankfurt
www.ontosverlag.com
info@ontosverlag.com